Samantha Abr

THE COMPLETE PLAYER

Samantha Abrams

THE COMPLETE PLAYER

A Neurological Description of the Love Game

Between the Player and his Mark

Written by Samantha Abrams

DEDICATION

I dedicate this book first to Dr. Dale VanderPutten. It took some twenty years for me realize how much pain I caused him. This book is my apology.

I also dedicate this book to Greggory who taught me a painful yet valuable lesson; one that I can now effectively impart to my daughters. For these reasons, I have profited.

Table of Contents

PREFACE

Generally, I'm not a very serious person. About 80% of everything I say or do is performed for my own amusement. The remaining 20% is a mix between amusing others and performing necessities like bathing, paying bills and rearing children. I do my best to incorporate creativity and amusement into my lifestyle so I laugh an awful lot, maybe too much and I thoroughly enjoy making others laugh. It all stems from having a meticulously flawed history so in my tumultuous experiences I've learned to find humor in everything. Chris Rock said it best in a 2016 interview with Essence magazine, "A perfect life makes horrible art." He's right. I come from poverty, dysfunction and abuse of all kinds and yet, although there are parts of my childhood that are blocked from my memory, I do recall a consistent chime of humor. I remember laughing; even at the most terrible events. Growing up in the projects, even if we didn't have money for groceries, we laughed as we ate pan-fried flour cakes, pretending they were delicious. If my brother flunked out of the fourth grade, we laughed. Once we got evicted and sat around a seedy motel room filled to the brim with all our poor-people apartment clutter most of which was stuffed into plastic trash bags, not including my hamster, whose cage was placed safely on the floor and I'm sorry but that shit was funny. We all laughed! It was equally as insane as it was therapeutic because thank goodness we could still laugh. How much worse should misery be that the poor and dysfunctional shouldn't laugh at their misfortune? What else are they supposed to laugh at?

The legend, Keenen Ivory Wayans defined comedy to me once. He said, "Comedy is reaching into a tragedy and finding the funny inside." The next time you are cracking up at your favorite comedian; consider what you're laughing at. I guarantee it won't be at someone's good fortune so I expect that although the subject matter herein is serious and you and I both may be in some degree of emotional pain, I'll find a way to put it all in clear perspective and hopefully make you laugh out loud. It would be impossible to explain certain concepts without including some fairly complicated biology (especially neurology) so I'll do my best to pear the science down to smart and simple anecdotes while keeping the jokes as stupid as possible.

In short, at thirty-eight years old, I was recently divorced with two young daughters, ages five and two. The last three years of my marriage, I had been a stay-at-home mom and my youngest was developing special needs so I felt obligated to continue staying at home and applied for financial assistance through the State of California. After nearly eight years of a loveless marriage I was broke, depressed, desperate and unbeknownst to me, extremely vulnerable. Then I met a man, fell in love and eventually found myself suffering through the worst kind of heartbreak I had ever known.

He and I met conducting a small business deal. I am an artist and needed his permission to sell a pencil rendering of him that I never ended up selling. I framed a copy for him which I believe he still hangs on his living room wall. What started as casual advanced to sexual within a year. Before I knew it, reality hit and I realized that I had fallen deeply in love with him. The trouble was he seemed to have had no feelings for me at all; as in zero, null, zilch and how the hell did this happen? I was merely his play thing and yet for many moons, I had no idea.

Admittedly, I was no amateur at being the play thing. Hell, before marriage and at intervals during my lavish drinking career, I was the perfect play thing and most times preferred the "no-strings" relationship. For years, I had been an emotionally detached drug addict and a drunk with no expressive availability for humans, including myself. I was a complete savage; never heartbroken. Finally, after living and loving a little, getting married, having children, divorcing, learning how to trust people and moreover getting sober from alcohol; it *almost* felt like I had some clarity. Naturally, I figured I'd try again and give emotional connectivity another shove. I wasn't after a husband this time. I wanted a consistent sexual-emotional connection with a man. What happened however, was the first time a man had treated me in a way that made me feel something existed that didn't; namely his feelings for me. It turned out, there was nothing there; at least none that I could reasonably detect. Therefore, he will be forever remembered as my first player.

During those early weeks of painful discovery about my lover, I recalled writing a specific journal entry which has become the lot of this book's preface. My warning is that this particular section comes from raw, painful emotion which is the motivation behind the creation of this book. Although the nature of this book's content is raw, its introduction does not reflect the type of language or emotion used throughout subsequent chapters. My sole purpose in writing this book is to explain through behavioral neuroscience what happens on both sides of a relationship where the love emotion has been tampered with carelessly. For me, finding this explanation was my ticket out of all the pain and disappointment but it wasn't just about moving on. At the heart of it, I had to figure out how and why I had allowed this to happen. My player's nickname for me was "Sam-Sam" and I could not, should not, would not let this happen again. Sam, I am.

"Books!" I thought. Deep in the midst of my broken heart, I remembered books and sought them out. I searched and searched and read books on how to play a player, how to be a player, how to not get played, how to play the game and even found a book on how to play the game without playing the game. The hell? I spent at least $185 and about six months of reading articles and books; all of which were a crock. None of it made any sense because none of it, and I mean none of it was based in science. Although it was tough discovering that none of the hours I had spent reading would be of any immediate help to me, I was encouraged because as the book I wanted did not exist, I felt somehow commissioned by the gods to write it. How dare someone sit down for any long period of time to write a book on how to fix your broken heart without mentioning your broken brain? The audacity! Everything we do and feel is linked to our brains. My goal was heightened. I had to take a hard look at my antennas and learn how to read in between the lines, make sense of all the dysfunction I had experienced, reconcile it all through science and then write about it. Writing this book made me feel like a super hero coming to the aid of every woman on earth that has ever had her love emotion meddled with. Introducing, the spectacular and mind-boggling ill-adventures of *Miss Kiss My Grits*!

I changed how I researched and went in just like any normal person doing my best to sift through case studies with Google dictionary a click away, sorting through thick vocabulary just to get the gist. I kept piercing through the medical terms and mathematics. It was difficult and time consuming but luckily, I already had some background in neuroscience. My second daughter had been diagnosed with Autism which caused me first to research the brain on a cognitive level. At the time, I only needed to understand how we learn and perform skills so that I could teach my daughter effectively. After my heartbreak, I sought out to find out how the brain affects us emotionally but I couldn't nail it down to just one science. Was it psychology or neurology? I took a course in psychology; which lead me to anthropology, the study of human culture and societies; which lead me back again to neurology which caused me to take a course in genetics, which pointed back to neurology then over to molecular biology, nutrition and so on. I'm still learning but the big take away is this; all of it is connected and all of it revolves around our brains.

Whereas sciences like psychology and anthropology lend effective studies that add valuable information to understanding intent and emotion; like all science, social sciences are built from associative theories and their findings are formed through interpretations of behavioral tendencies and odd scientific correlations. Essentially; really, really good guesses. Probability of human tendency is full of variables and can be debated, on the other hand, results from a brain scan; namely, functional magnetic resonance imaging or fMRI, cannot be argued with.

Therefore, *this* book about womanizing is unique because the theories herein are firmly constructed around and within neurological research and its psychological implications. With little influence from my emotional experience, I analyze personal events under a scientific microscope to explain neurologically what happened to me, to him and countless others. That said; this was my uninformed and emotionally scattered journal entry written on a sad, cold February afternoon which documents the first of the many, many attempts I made at leaving my player alone.

"It's been six months and I finally wised up. Last week something tragic occurred to me. The man I am in love with is a complete player and I am his play thing. I have been in agony ever since. I had no idea it would feel like this because I did not know I had fallen this far... not until it started hurting. I have never been played in the past because even the raunchy men I dealt with had been man enough to be honest about their wants. Hell, I was raunchy too and knew that a piece of ass was the exchange; mine for his. I knew it therefore it was easy. Even in my twenties when I had been the side chick and in love, he made it clear where I stood saying, "I love you but I can't leave my family." We were both wrong but I stayed and enjoyed myself for three more years because I wanted to. Right or wrong, I chose it, lived through and learned from it. I was 19 then and today at age 38, I know better. Either way, we were adults and neither of us played the game of deception which aligns my current heartache parallel to the rape I experienced as a teenager. Oddly, it feels similar. This man made me believe he was someone else. If I had known, I would not have made the choice to touch him. In retrospect, it was like giving a complete stranger a blowjob accidentally and yet voluntarily. Twice!

My eight-year marriage ended and here I am, a year and a half later drowning in tears over two blowjobs and a broken heart. What the fuck? Love sick is no joke. I feel like I have the flu. Everything is overwhelming. I need to do my daughters' hair and I'm struggling to find the energy through this exhausting grief. I am in sorrow. Never has my anguish over a man been this degrading and cutting. My brain feels broken. My daughters are sad for me and I need to hurry up and get over this mess so I can be fully present for them. Meanwhile, I can't even tell them what's wrong. They had no idea I was in love. Neither did I. I'm pleading with my creator to expedite this pain. This is too much to handle for very long.

I feel sorry for the woman that stays, trying to make a man feel something he can't. For her, this anguish is prolonged. I'm just so confused about why someone would go through such trouble for two blowjobs. He invested at least four consistent months of kissing and cuddling, checking in, singing to me, kissing my forehead, holding my hand, taking me out, making me feel special, etc. I've known this guy for a year and a half. It just seems like so much work when there are so, so many women available to him because [of his status]. But he chose to entertain my fragile-ass emotions. Why? Why me? Why was I so interesting and enticing? What kind of sick game was he intending to play with me? Or had the motherfucker given it any thought?

He told me he was all talk and no bark; a "fraidy cat"; a dummy when it comes to women. I told him how I felt about him from the beginning and again each time my feelings grew. Finally, I told him if he did not feel the same that he should walk away. Then I told him goodbye and yet he still called me with nothing to say. I'm convinced, he was just checking to see if he could get a third blowjob. It felt evil and hurt something awful.

It must take a delicate plan and acute energy to get someone to fall in love with you just for fun. This kind of thing doesn't just happen by accident. What the fuck? It can't. It seems as such a tremendous performance; a strategic act that is practiced and refined. Contrary to popular belief, mere sex couldn't have been his goal because there is an ample amount of easy sex out in the world. Loose women flock to him. His goal must have been to play me; to conquer my body *and* my mind. He is a *complete* player because clearly, he wanted both and he wanted them fully with no reserve for my emotional safety. He won't tolerate me unless I'm happy, smiling and ready to suck dick. I am not allowed to complain about the way he treats and neglects my feelings. I feel stuck between a rock and a hard place because if I withhold my kindness, I fear I may lose him and yet I know if I extend him kindness and love, he will trample over it. On one hand, letting him go is clearly my best-case scenario but it's tricky. I love him. I have to first get rid of this stupid love and let my heart break into pieces just to see if it feels better on the other side.

So, I forgive him even though this hurts like hell. I have to forgive and realize that he is in own kind of pain; either by his own fault or with the help of others who failed him. At any rate, he is certainly a man that is troubled; not because of how he treats me but because of his ancillary lifestyle. Living with consequences is an unyielding principle that cannot be challenged. To the individual, the internal struggles which define the reasons behind merciless behaviors are often punishment enough. Therefore eventually, whether he is conscious of his own malevolence, he is feeling or will feel his own form of regret for the way he treats people. (I don't feel singled-out.) Today, I am accepting that it is not my job nor is it possible to enforce my offender's remorse. I've never had the stomach for revenge. I'm used to people disappointing me. At its core, revenge is futile because it is impossible to control a person's level of accountability. It is a complete waste of time and energy because it does nothing to progress your own healing. From a very young age, I have been living my life in a state of self-loathing and today, I finally understand the gravity of this need to love myself. Suddenly the issue is urgent. I have to get out of this mess. I don't know what it looks like but I am dead set on finding out. I'm tired. I need rest from this prison of mistrust. I need to find out what's wrong with me. Why did I let him in?"

Finally, I found myself over forty and wholeheartedly addicted but not to drugs or alcohol this time. I was addicted to a man. I continued to see him after writing this journal entry for several years. How could I not? I was a troubled soul, fully in love with all of his pleasure, messiness and dysfunction. It had been five years of knowing him and four long years of loving him and for what reasons I strived to seek out. Two blowjobs had turned into a twice a month habit. How could I have written over a hundred pages of neurological analysis about this subject and yet, still be within his hold, just as hurt and shocked? What the hell was wrong with me? How could I be so smart and yet so stupid? He was not always nice to me in fact I had to demand any form of respect from him. I'm convinced, any resemblance of respect was an act he put on just so he could get what he wanted; that is, my craving of his body and acceptance. It was twisted and insane and like with an illicit drug, I was stuck even though underneath it all, I knew the relationship was toxic. Admittedly, like many women in my position, I didn't know what a healthy relationship looked like.

"I stopped seeing him," I would say. "Why is it different this time?" my girlfriend would ask and I always had an answer; "Because he's still numb," or "Because he's not nice," or "Because his lifestyle is too much." Somehow, none of my landings stuck. I needed to land elsewhere; in a place that would not give me a loophole; that is, the hope of him waking up from his emotional slumber – as I saw it – and loving me back. Eventually, I blamed his cold-heartedness on his addiction to drugs, cleared myself from any fault in the matter and tried my best to move on. It was a sloppy, cold and necessary step. I didn't give up on him I concluded. I gave up trying to control his health and emotions through the giving of affection and blow jobs. There is no mathematical formula for such nonsense and the logic comes strictly from dysfunction. For the time I spent involved with him, an acute uncertainty always lingered about his feelings for me. Bottom line, he never told me. Both my grandmother and mother had once said, "If a man cares about you, you'll know it." Ultimately, I asked him in an email. The result; he gave no reply at all. He ignored me and I did not follow up. I was equally as devastated as I was grateful to have no answer because it gave me the courage to land somewhere else.

How could I have missed his transition from the gentlemen to the crook? What type of morbid trick did my brain play on me? How could I have misinterpreted disrespect for love? How could he not care one bit that I was hurt? And why do I even care if he cares? I'm more mature than this so how could I have been so blind? I could not yet answer any of these piercing questions so I continued my research.

I read books on the science of neurology, anatomy and biochemistry. I learned about important scientific theories and read full case studies from unsurpassed universities. I took medical courses online; even a physics course. I became obsessed. I peeled through hundreds of pages of neuroscience studies, publications and articles to try and understand what encourages the type of dynamic between the user and giver. What I discovered initially were more questions. Do givers all possess or experience the same type of vulnerability? Is there a fundamental physical or neurological trait or personal insecurity that all users share? Could there be some detectable gene, environmental influence or neurological profile that might indicate a person's susceptibility to falling in love with a user or falling in love at all? I had to find answers and set out on what began as a quest for understanding and ended in a passage to healing, forgiveness and spiritual enlightenment. In the end, I gained a valuable truth about my brain, his brain and the synergy between human nature and circumstances.

This book is primarily written to the player's mark, to inform her about the player and about the pain they both suffer and cause. It is not meant to expose either in a negative light more than it is to show them both within a scientific scope. We explore the pains and dysfunction plaguing both sides of this unscrupulous game. The purpose of this book is to reach all those affected by this love sport and help them shed some light on what has happened in order to help them heal. It is my hope that it will serve to help and not harm, however, I fully understand the clear risk that some players may read this book and strengthen their game. Decidedly, I will unrelentingly hold out hope that more potential marks will read these pages than will players, therefore empowering safety to the unsuspecting. Additionally, I'll hold out a great hope for my two daughters that I will never have to wipe the type of tears from their faces that I cried for a man named Greggory.

CHAPTER 1 | THE PSYCHOLOGY OF THE GAME

The brain is like a two-edged sword; having the ability to both encourage and frustrate our most remarkable endeavors.

Let us first level the overall playing field on this subject before defining the game. It is important to understand that the participants in this sport are engaged in two different games, on two different fields with two totally separate sets of rules. The game here is one between hearts. The player seeks to win hearts without giving his own. The mark seeks after an exchange of hearts; hers for his. The playing field here is science and especially the relationship of how the brain affects the way we perceive everything.

The participants in this love game are men and women and neither walks through life looking through the same types of goggles. We are very different, in fact there are a myriad of articles, scientific studies and books published about how contrastingly males and females experience life and love. Barring all the complicated scientific stuff, the easiest way to summarize it all is to say this; men and women are dissimilar as hell. It is vital that we recognize our differences so we can interact with and balance them in a way that coincides with nature, emotional health and more importantly *reality*.

When we, the commoner, exclude ourselves from scientific knowledge, we become susceptible to peculiar superstitions. That is, when we don't understand stuff, we guess. We pretend we can read our lovers' minds and predict their reactions. We're disappointed if their reactions are not what we expect and sometimes become hurt, depressed or downright angry when we guess wrong. Hell, turn the tables and we can even justify our own bad behavior when we guess about our motives and environment. Immaturity is often the result of having a dull consideration of one's own perceptions and opinions. Having a basic understanding of the brain, psychology and even genetics means you better understand how to interact with the world and especially the people around you. Limiting your understanding of the human mind is like eating cereal with a fork. You're just not getting the full range of the life experience. If you're constantly expecting the world to think like you then you are clearly missing the point and life becomes much more complicated and less enjoyable. Men and women do not; I repeat, do not think alike.

As humans, genetically, we are all about 99.9% identical. As a species, we are extremely similar and yet the .1% that differentiates us, combined with our unique environments, causes us to develop as individuals totally distinct in our appearance and thinking. When it comes to male and female interaction, the scale of psychological differences is even more astounding. Once you can grasp how the human mind works, it makes it a lot easier to manage relationships of all kinds. Trying to understand relationships without a basic grasp of how the sexes differ is impossible. It would be like trying to predict how subatomic particles colliding at light speed would behave without a background in quantum physics. It would be mere guesswork; in fact, you wouldn't dare try. Some folks know more about how their car works than how their body and mind work. It is counterintuitive to operate within our bodies without some strategic inquiring; namely reading this book, Google searching or asking lots of questions at the doctor's office.

If you are the kind of nerd that I am, it might be fun to take an online medical course. What you'll find will fascinate you. For example, it is in fact true that psychological influences like being in an abusive or safe childhood environment can affect how your genes are expressed. That is, how you think changes the way you develop. Absolutely fascinating! Equally as impressive; your diet also has a direct effect on your genetics and brain function; aka your way of thinking. In turn, your genetics and thinking patterns will feedback onto what you choose to eat and the environments you create for yourself. We all have this internal cycle at play. We are our own biological and emotional ecosystem and keeping it balanced means understanding how it works. This is especially appropriate when a woman is trying to sift through the quagmire of emotional and sexual ties to people who do not value her.

Before delving too deep into the scientific facets between players and marks, it is important to note that this book is no inference that women do not play men's emotions because it is clearly a trend for some women to string lovers along for their money, sex, power or fame; having no emotional attachments to the men they use. Additionally, gay and lesbian relationships can also mirror these similar codependent dynamics. Nevertheless, for the sake of ease, going forward I will refer to the male as the "player" and to the female as his "mark" since this is the specific research that I have devoted time to. Should I decide to pick apart the dynamics between the female player and the men they hurt or respectively dysfunctional gay, lesbian or transgender relationships, it will be a separate piece of work certainly with a completely different research model.

Additionally, this is in no way a blame game to decide who is at fault; the player or his mark. The point is to shed some light on how your brain and body process perception and emotion so you can transcend it and create a more acceptable reality. Whether you can explain away bad behavior by use of clairvoyance, fluffy self-help books or hardcore science, there is one thing that holds true; we are driven to explain it. Bad behavior just doesn't go unobserved and forgotten. We obsess over hurt feelings and the people, places and things that we perceive caused them. The purpose of this book is to help you overcome the *perception* of emotional pain by giving you a more than basic understanding of how it got there. A scientific approach, is always more sound than mere guessing. I hate fluffy self-help books. I hope you do too. So, let us lay a few groundwork concepts before defining the game and its regulations.

SUPERSTITION

B. F. Skinner was a behavioral psychologist famous for inventing very clever and curious experiments that explain behavior regarding the experience of reward. Reward can come in many forms; sex, food, money, etc. One notable experiment demonstrated the development of superstition and how humans speculate about how the world works around them. He analyzed how we put together stories when we don't know the whole picture and he demonstrated this using pigeons and a food reward.

Ten birds were placed in a box individually. Every minute without fail, a pellet of food was dropped into the center of each box. Two of the birds learned very quickly that the food would drop every interval without any interaction from them. (If I were a bird, I'd like to think I'd be one of these two.) Interestingly, the other eight birds all formed a fierce superstition of what they thought caused the food to drop. Some would nod their heads in a peculiar way, others walked around in a circle while another paced from side to side; all in an attempt to produce a new food pellet. These eight birds had all figured that whatever activity they were doing just before the pellet dropped might have had something to do with it having dropped. Eventually, if they kept performing the odd behavior, the food would appear. It seemed to work like a charm. Skinner hypothesized that this is how humans form superstition. We speculate. Some people wholeheartedly believe that when they wear a certain pair of underwear, they'll generally *do* better. As a result, they continue to wear the same underwear for days believing it will help their chances in life as opposed to say; itchy private parts? The bottom line here is that if the pigeons possessed the knowledge that a new pellet would drop without their involvement, they could and would cease the unnecessary behaviors.

This is kind of how dysfunction works. People get into practices that they believe will help their chances at love and success. If the habits they formed early were unhealthy, they continue in these unnecessary behaviors and often without the discovery of some very vital amalgamation of knowledge, people cannot transcend their unhealthy lifestyles. In relationships, if you don't understand how you or your lover's brain works, you will create your own superstition to what caused both your behaviors. You become prone to misinterpretations and miscommunications which can lead to a degradation of your emotional health. We become like the pigeon bouncing back and forth trying to get a reaction from our love interests and even from ourselves. Sound familiar? Pick a different pigeon. This concept is where I began to learn that my personal issues with being played were less about what my player had finagled and more about the environment that I created and entertained; all because I was uninformed.

SEX IS CHEMISTRY

There are a few playing fields in the game between players and their marks but of them all, sex is certainly one of the heavy hitters. On a basic level, most women and men will eventually experience sexual desire and form strategies to acquire sex at some point in their lifetime. That is to say; it is typically an integral part of life and especially on this alluring and adventurous journey between the mark and her player. Sex is important and yet most folks interpret much of the pleasure of sex and sexual pursuit in a myriad of different ways. Sexual pleasure can make you feel connected to people on a deep level and can outright feel like love, respect and value. Let's face it. We've all been there. Sometimes we're in good hands, sometimes we're not. There are a ton of emotional connections made in the brain during sex that cause a bundle of responses both physical and mental. Interpreting them wisely means first understanding that sex and sexual selection have an awful lot to do with chemistry.

While most women are certainly sexual, due to their hormonal chemistry and cultural influences they are very different in mating behaviors than males and the criteria by which they select their mates. The human female typically chooses her mate with expectations of long-term involvement and emotional connectivity. Occasionally, she may choose less emotional connection with a more long-term physical strategy, but rarely will a woman in her right mind choose the one-night-stand. There have been occasions where I have chosen it, but psychologically and physiologically, neither were balanced decisions because on 100% of those occasions, I was drunk out of my mind. It is no secret about the power of alcohol to alter one's chemistry by turning inhibitions off and sexy *on*. If a woman is sober, she is generally more selective about who she lays with. Women choose a mate that fits her specific needs and men choose based on availability.

Many mammals share unique pair bonding or mating rituals within species. Humans share mating instincts but there also exist huge variations. The male often feels compelled to take up with any female that is available and showing an interest in him sexually. Men differ in how they mate and yet while the goal is sexual fulfillment and masculinity, for different sets of reasons some men are aggressive while others are not. Some are looking for sex only, others for relationships and others for marriage. Some men secure the main squeeze along with a few side-dishes, whereas others exclusively commission prostitutes in a rejection-free zone. Some cheat, some don't and a small percentage of men rarely if ever pursue sex. Females can also mirror these variances so while we ease you into the subject of love-gaming, let us first establish that there are no averages. When it comes to love and sexual attraction; a gigantic network of influence is at play, namely compatibility, selection, chemistry, circumstances and mental capacity are all crucial; not to mention being in the right-wrong place at the right-wrong time. We are bound by our culture and chemistry which have an undeniable influence on where in love and life we end up. Not all players will use the same strategies and generally humans are not all slated for the same romantic destiny. Heads up! Your situation is unique based on the chemistry you've created.

SEX AND MONOGAMY

Behavioral studies on prairie voles are popular among scientists because these rodents' mating habits reflect the human notion of monogamy. This species will choose one mate for life and even with death, the surviving vole will not pair bond with another. When scientists experimented on the voles with vasopressin (the male "love" hormone) it became apparent that when this hormone's receptors are suppressed to extreme levels, the male voles not only fail to pair bond with females, they become promiscuous. If a promiscuous male vole is then administered accelerants to his vasopressin receptors, he becomes monogamist. Additionally, using a certain species of mice, other case studies in the United States observed that some of these mice have monogamous behaviors while others are promiscuous within the same species. When their receptors were compared, a connection was drawn to the hormone vasopressin in each group of mice. The study found that unfaithful male mice have far fewer receptors than the faithful mice.

This suggests that in human males, susceptibility to monogamy lies in the number and vitality of not only his vasopressin receptors but also the levels of vasopressin his body generates; among other unknown environmental factors. Theoretically, it would therefore not be wise to fall in love with a man whose brain naturally produces low vasopressin or whose vasopressin receptors are functioning below average. Essentially, a man's susceptibility for romantic love lies in his vasopressin receptiveness; which can also be affected by his diet, genes, behavior or drug use. And even if his receptors are intact, there are a myriad of socioeconomic reasons some people or prairie voles for that matter would, could and should never pair bond. To be plain, everyone's chemistry and needs won't match.

Women know innately that men are sexual and expect to be pursued. What they don't know is how a man's pursuit is positioned and short of scanning his brain, ordering his blood work combined with a real sharp case of clairvoyance, her only way to be sure she is in a pair-bonding situation is to risk some degree of emotional investment and wait to see how her love interest behaves. This unfortunately, is nature's nasty little hormonal trick on the female. The upside is that women are emotional creatures and have ample experience at dealing with disappointment. Heartbreak is inevitable and a familiar emotion for females. This learned skill starts at adolescence when she begins falling in love for the first time and very easily. This is partly why women can strategically move away from love more seamlessly than men. A man in love that is heartbroken is a man with a foreign problem and therefore a deeper kind of hurt is at play. The female super power is to develop as emotionally resilient; having the ability to be both soft and hard-hearted; simultaneously. Hard-heartedness in emotional relationships is a matter of female instinct and survival that compensates for the ability to become soft or vulnerable. It is a protection from her unending and chemically driven desire to endure the risks of pair bonding.

COGNITIVE VS. EMOTIONAL RESPONSES

For the mark, this section may either be upsetting or a complete and utter relief. I am going to attempt to scientifically explain why the mark's player does not care that she is heartbroken. Understanding hurtful human responses makes it a lot easier to accept them. Often it is the uncertainty that we fear. It is the *not knowing* that causes our deepest and most prolonged pain. When a couple has a child go missing, they will writhe night after night for years wondering if their child is alive or dead and if they are alive, whether they are being hurt or cared for. If an officer visits their home to deliver horrible news that the child has been found deceased, suddenly their brains will have an answer to the unanswerable and can settle into some subsequent course of action; that is, processing their loss and healing their pain.

The goal is relief from the pain. We need to settle somewhere in order to move past a broken heart however, our tendency is to hold onto a morbid hope that our player felt something or that he will eventually come around to loving us. I say morbid because this dream of being loved by our player is dead yet we resurrect it time and time again; each time re-rigging our pain. If like me, you never knew whether his feelings were involved, then accept that they were not so that you can have a ground on which to move about. Your other alternative is to continue pretending he loves you and stand still inside your pain. The latter is quite ridiculous.

To fully understand my attempt to explain away the player's emotional accountability, one must first understand the clinical difference between how the brain processes both cognition and emotion. Cognition is essentially how you *think* about something and emotion is how you *feel* about something. For example, you are cognitive that your toast is burned but your emotive response is frustration and to the brain each is a different process but each is based on the other. There is a loop happening with automatic and controlled neural action inside the platform of neurology and moral compass. Recent studies have shown a clear connection between cognition and emotions asserting that previous theories about which comes first could be wrong. It was previously theorized that emotion is an automatic reaction to stimulus and therefore controlled cognitive action is required to stave the emotion or stop it from continuing; therefore, paving the way for clear thinking and moral decision making. Today, we are aware that the two play an almost simultaneous role in moral judgment.

Cognition and emotion are not two separate entities in the brain just as the brain has no real core but is a cohesive network with each of its functions having a great deal of power over the overall processes. Moral action is therefore connected to cognitive and emotional patterns in our brains and we form emotional opinions as well those that have been reliably proven through evidences we can observe; aka cognition. When there is a lack of evidence, we can still form an emotional opinion about a topic based on what our related cognitive opinions have been all our lives. For example, if your player has gone missing for a week, you can and will certainly form an emotional opinion; namely, feelings of abandonment. On another hand, you will also use those emotional values and neurons to form more cognitive or evidence-based opinions; for instance, "He does this all the time," or, "He's probably hung-over or drunk." Each time, the mark refines her space of action around this procedure. Meanwhile, the player too has faith in his moral space that says, "I do this all the time and she never asks questions so everything is okay." Both make a cognitive and emotional decision to not care. Cognition and emotion cannot be separated as the science of psychology suggested in its more primitive phases in the early and mid-1900's and before the invention of the MRI; notably this was also back during a time when race-killing concentration camps were a fad; all in the name of genetic science. Stupid is as stupid does. But I digress.

Voluntary action and brain function can become so repetitive it becomes involuntary. Same goes true for emotive responses. The player is so well practiced at being avoidant and deceitful that in many ways he has become accustom to a low level of accountability and therefore it no longer feels like a moral decision to ignore his mark. He may feel remorse against circumstances he causes that do not relate to his sexual encounters however, as his frontal lobe begins to sculpt its space of actions around emotions, his moral compass regards sex-related malevolence and their justifications as fully logical. In other words, with enough practice, a player can become an expert at not giving a fat baby's ass about anything that gets in the way of his sex life.

In an interview a day before his execution, which eventually aired years later on a Christian talk-radio show called Dr. James Dobson's Family Talk; infamous serial killer, Ted Bundy, explained the thinking behind his history of serial rape, murder and necrophilia. He talked about having found very violent pornography in a neighborhood dumpster as a teenager and went into detail about how gruesome the images were. After viewing its contents, he sought out more materials and eventually developed an obsessive fantasy life around violent sex. Eventually he became sexually charged enough by his fantasy life that he began to strategize about how he would go about making them a reality. He planned how he would choose and murder his victims. His brain had associated sexual pleasure with violent images and his fantasies of acting out his fantasies lead him to doing them. After his first murder he admitted to feeling deep guilt and shame but he would simply fantasize sexually to cover his pain. About six months after getting away with his first murder, he did it again. This time he admitted his guilt and shame were still heavy but said it was easier to deal with. Eventually, he confessed to becoming desensitized to the guilt as he continued to murder. His brain was essentially adapting its moral compass to accommodate his actions. He was becoming an expert at not caring.

Before his death, he asserted his overall guilt about what he had done, but this was after years in prison reading the bible and counseling with prison pastors. His last interview was exclusive to Dr. James Dobson who is a staunchly conservative Christian. Religion became Bundy's new compass and with enough conditioning and training, his brain readapted and he again experienced guilt. His values had shifted and according to him, his associations with violent images and sexual arousal, although still present, had been decreased to some extent. His newly acquired moral associations reshaped many of his cognitive and emotional associations to the degree that he could articulate a clear and intellectual progression of his evil behaviors. This is certainly not to say that prison preachers can fix serial killers or that an fMRI can quantify evil. It is, however, to say that we live in a world wherein people do evil stuff and their brains train them to do more evil until something or someone stops them; like a prison sentence for example. In order to stop offensive behavior, an individual must be triggered to have both a cognitive and emotional realization that things have to change.

With the player, although his offenses clearly cannot compare to serial murder, the sculpting of his moral space of action is a process that applies to all humans. His patterns, outcomes, behaviors and all of his history have shaped and formed the relationships between his associations with people and his cognitive and emotional values. In other words, the player and his marks over time have taught him how to not feel because he has survived just fine without it and without suffering a negative outcome. His only romantic consequence is that he loses some of his marks which to him is not motivating because he is already accustomed to not caring. Having a heart for his mark is not a part of his strategy in fact, caring is the anti-strategy because it requires his energy. It doesn't make sense for him to become emotional. If he loses her, he sees it as an opportunity to replace her. He does not consider her side of things. If he experienced excellent sex with her, it will fuel the excitement in his quest to find another one like her. It entices his game and gives further definition in his plan to find the perfect mark; one that will never complain, never leave him and will continually provide him sexual and emotional favors.

EMOTIONAL ATTACHMENT VS. DETACHMENT

The coldest implication for the mark is her sexual-emotional attachment. This is the final and only byproduct of the player's game. He wins by her losing a little. Causing her to fall in love by some degree, he succeeds in making and keeping her loyal to him sexually. Philosophically, it is a most selfish endeavor. Once the relationship is over, his mark is left with a deep emotional and sexual attachment. No matter her progression, she has been affected. Dissipating these attachments is mentally painful and physically exhausting. During this transition, the brain causes a psychological pressure but there is a tough physiological battle at hand as well. The evolution into sexual detachment in the midst of deep emotional attachment is very difficult to endure for both men and women. The mark is left to endure this suffering alone when the relationship ends. Perhaps not worth mentioning, the player suffers only a minor inconvenience. This lopsided end should not be a distraction to the mark. It is unwise to muddle in the discomfort of unfairness because truthfully, life has never been fair. No one reputable ever said it was supposed to be. She should focus instead on solving her problem; that is, detaching emotionally from a person who regards her as mere sexual convenience.

The brain processes emotional pain and physical pain differently yet in some ways very much the same. More factors are at play in the brain as it processes emotional pain than are present when experiencing physical pain. Physical pain only occasionally brings about emotional pain yet emotional pain will almost inevitably bring about physical ailments. This dynamic is equally as fascinating to laymen as it is evident to scientists who also know that the human neurological experience of social rejection and physical pain are both rooted in exactly the same regions of the brain. In fact, physical pain caused by emotion stimuli can become so severe that one can actually die of a broken heart.

This condition is called *stress cardiomyopathy* and is caused by intense emotional or physical stress and leads to rapid and irreversible cardiac dysfunction. When emotional stress has triggered enough cortisol into the bloodstream, the heart can become overworked and its muscle tissue or myocardium can become weakened. These tiny string-like muscle tissues are exactly what are referred to when we talk about our "heart strings". The term is in no way figurative. A pulling on these strings is literally what is happening when we endure emotional suffering. Myocardium, like a band of field soldiers, carries strength in numbers but once their protective frontline begins to diminish, the enemy can rush in quickly and succession folds swiftly with a devastating domino effect. So is the collapse of love in the heart. Its affects come quickly and can be shocking. Once myocardium have been compromised it can cause lethal ventricular arrhythmias, ventricular rupture and acute heart failure; all deadly of course. Stress cardiomyopathy might be caused by constant anxiety, the death of a loved one or the ending of a relationship and is therefore more commonly known as *broken heart syndrome*.

Detaching emotionally literally strains the mind and body. It is a gradual process and success requires consistency in pattern of thought and behavior. An individual must practice forcing themselves to stop unhealthy thinking cycles to get past the painful feelings. Obsession over a lost love relationship can feel the same as being happily and mutually in love, in fact the same regions of the brain activate and in similar ways. These regions, when stimulated can motivate a person to passionately seek their love object and can cause them to spend most of the day thinking about them. Obsessive behaviors cause familiar chemical imbalances which also create a strain on your physical body. Under these kinds of stresses, your heart beats differently, your breathing changes and so do your sleep and eating patterns. Your sleep and eating patterns then begin to change the way you think, weakening your resolve. In your weakness you begin to seek those familiar chemical imbalances; aka obsessing over your love interest. After all, you and your brain both know it gives you pleasure.

To overcome emotional urges, one must create a new, healthy chemical balance around your object of obsession. Your brain literally needs go through a withdrawal while it refrains from abnormal or unwanted emotions. It needs this so that it can deprogram and resume normalized emotional activity. Interestingly, attachment and detachment are the building blocks of addiction as addicts mentally attach to and detach from their drug of choice. Similarly, so too will the mark toggle between moving towards and away from her lover. We've all been there. It's that love-hate; get-out-come-here type of feeling but again, the key to progress is consistency. The mark must make a constant decision to avoid neurological sexual connections to her player. This means refraining from listening to love songs, scrolling through pictures of him on social media, texting, writing texts and not sending them, calling, emailing, thinking about and finally masturbating to her love object. Once she begins practicing better chemicals, everything begins to fall back into optimal working order. She will eventually crave the unhealthy chemical profiles less and less.

The alternative would be to feed your obsession, and this is unsafe. Obsessive love is never good, in fact it isn't love but more a type of entitlement to others; as in, "You're my property and you're wrong for not loving me." This is a dangerous way to think. No one owes you love but you. Detach from the people that don't love you and move onward in a position of self-love. Relying on others to keep you happy can cause dangerous consequences like stalking and even murder. My second to oldest brother is serving a life sentence in a North Carolina prison for killing his ex-girlfriend in front of both of her sons. Her name was Tonya Boyd and my brother was 100% not in love with her. He was obsessed. He killed her and shot one of her sons in the face. Her son survived. He shot them because she would not get back together with him two months after the breakup. It was an incredible disaster and tragedy. If you are angry and having thoughts of harming yourself or others, get help and talk to someone about it immediately. Hurting someone will make your problems worse and affect more people than you can imagine.

VULNERABILITY

By definition, vulnerability is a state of being susceptible to physical or emotional harm. Periods of vulnerability typically occur after traumatic loss of people, places or things. Its evidence is manifested by displays of weakness and submission. This explains why after experiencing traumatic life events, we get all clingy and chaotic and maneuver through tough decisions foggy with clogged up filters. After emotional and physical trauma, good judgment becomes difficult. No one is immune to this phenomenon. Sally gets fired from her job. Sally eats too much cheesecake. Sally now feels fat and needs reassurance. Sally texts her ex-boyfriend. Sally is now pregnant. Often when we look back on our past mistakes, we fail to recall the loss we experienced prior to making the horrible decision. It is very possible that if you take an emotional inventory, you may find your terrible decisions happened after a terrible loss. I fell in love with my ex-husband within months of my oldest brother's death. I also fell in love with my player within months of my failed marriage. It felt like accidently having back-to-back babies.

Vulnerability and submission are a cause and effect relationship; that is, an event first weakens us and creates a state of vulnerability within which we perform submissive acts. Submission, by definition, is a yielding to or accepting of a superior force and is the byproduct of becoming vulnerable.

The force in this matter is the event that caused the state of being vulnerable. During vulnerable times, we are more likely to yield to our naivety against better judgment and make poor decisions to connect with people, places and things that are not healthy; all in an attempt to bring our brains back to what feels like "normal". These unhealthy connections eventually cause us more stress. Under continual stress, our brains will desperately seek to regain familiar neurological profiles; ones we know will cause us pleasure. It will remind us to revisit the same types of people, places and things that caused the mess in the first place. A cycle ensues between pain and pleasure. Interestingly, this mimics the pattern that occurs in the cycles of drug and alcohol addiction whose similarities we will explore in subsequent chapters.

When a child is brought to frustration, they are prone to give up and tantrum. The whole act is a desperate attempt to process uncomfortable feelings. As adults, we've learned to channel our frustration and our tantrums sound more like an internal whisper at 3:00 AM saying, "Just eat a whole bag of sugar cookies, hide the wrapper in the bathroom trash and go back to sleep." The first step was whatever uncomfortable event that has caused us to become vulnerable to sugar cookies. The next step is feeling obliged to a new, uncommon and yet temporary type of yielding or submitting to. We're talking about a new type of compromising, namely, providing sex, love and attention to a person who does not reciprocate; or gorging on sugar cookies when nobody's looking. We become vulnerable first then we submit to something we know full well is not a good idea; therefore, vulnerability has a deep connection to and rooting in submission.

The manifestation of unhealthy submission serves as some proof that the state of vulnerability exits. Only after rediscovering the wrapper you hid in the bathroom trash do you fully realize how ridiculous the whole plan was. This wrapper is your evidence of submitting to the cookies. The memory of the act of submission therefore becomes the gauge by which we measure how vulnerable we became.

Sometimes recalling a memory is your best defense against repeating bad behavior. For the sober alcoholic in a recovery program, remembering their last drunk is recommended often to strike the kind of fear of debacle that keeps them sober. In doing this, the alcoholic continually gauges and recalls his or her level of vulnerability to alcohol. Of course, one can become vulnerable without succumbing to the dangers it presents. Sober alcoholics are fully aware of their vulnerability and therefore cognitively avoid drinking. That is to say just because you feel vulnerable does not mean you are destined to screw up. Wise thinking can be our best weapon against dumb shit so while social science can predict such a state; the trick is to recognize when we arrive at vulnerability and while we're there, we should be damned careful.

Each of us has come under some kind of vulnerability at certain stages in our lives. These are points when life has become on some level too tough, draining of energy or traumatic. During these phases we often "give in" to divert energy once our emotional reserves become depleted. During and after a loss, we can become tolerant of and even invite nonsense into our lives; sometimes wittingly referred to as getting a case of the "fuck-its." It is as if we're saying to ourselves, "I'm too tired to deal with this. I'm going to turn my rationalization meter off for a few days while I regroup and eat these cookies." This is what vulnerability can feel like. We just don't have the energy to keep caring and adjust our boundaries sometimes in a not-so-healthy accommodation.

Vulnerability is the inauspicious backbone in the game between the player and his mark. If she is not vulnerable, he has no chance and the game is forfeited. One writer very cleverly wrote in a book called *Player Slayer*, "[Female] emotional detachment to the player is like a cross to the vampire." Simply put, if the mark is vulnerable, she is who the player is looking for. Coincidentally, the player's character also becomes who *she* is looking for. Her vulnerability is his hook. Without it, he cannot snare her. While a lack of vulnerability may not be the defining factor that deems her impervious to the player; on the other hand, her sense of confidence will most certainly prove her an impossible mark. A player's only strategy is to appeal to her vulnerabilities and therefore needs his mark to be compromised emotionally. If he can provide a sense of relief for some deep hurt she bears, he has an emotional hook. Without her vulnerability, he cannot play her because he has no other strategy and none of his available tactics will measure up. The one who is vulnerable wants to be rescued and anyone willing to merely appear to be chivalrous is a likely candidate for their hero.

If a woman is vulnerable, she can be extremely submissive. If she is not the right amount of submissive, the player's game has no chance to commence because again, he cannot draw his hand against her confidence. He must draw a card that will entice her but if self-assured; her long-term standards will be much higher than any he is willing to accommodate. She will require much because she is certain of who she was, is and will be. This is not an attractive mark. This is simply too much work. A player's game is to "hook" her, not to feed her in a healthy emotional progression and therefore has to quickly petition her submission and weaknesses or move on to the next mark.

In my case, I had lived my life virtually love avoidant, never fully emotionally attached to the men I dated. At age five, I was introduced to alcohol and sex of all kinds by a small group of teenagers lead by an adult male, all of which lived in our low-income project complex in North Carolina. My abuse was traumatic and ended at age seven when we moved away from that neighborhood. The sexual abuse stopped but I had picked up a mean alcohol habit. As I developed into a teenager, I also engaged in all kinds of drunken promiscuity and lived in a perpetual state of emotional fear; unless I was drunk. The booze helped me block emotion and by adulthood, I developed very thick, alcoholic skin to compensate for the constant fear. My memories are scattered and at age forty-three I still can't remember full seasons of my childhood. The chronology is all out of order and I often confuse middle school with high school. It is tough to separate all the blended memories; most of which remained a blur due to my fierce progression with alcoholism.

I met my ex-husband just one month before my oldest brother passed away in 2004. I fell in love with him during my first week of bereavement. My ex was also going through his own form of depression so he too was emotionally vulnerable. We were both feeling hopeless and desperate for love and admitted it to each other. It was pathetic. While we were dating, he let me talk to him about my past and to my astonishment, he accepted me. This felt like a miracle. I was living through a stage of life where I had been forced to recall the sexual abuse from my childhood and was trying to put it all together. For the first time, I was beginning to reconcile all my dysfunction. Prior to that, my only level of gauging was that the world seemed to disapprove of my behavior. I knew I wasn't normal, but I didn't know how to fix it.

Several months before I met my ex-husband, I had an epiphany. It all started at work when a girlfriend had heard I had "dated" three guys we worked with. The truth was there were four and I had not been on a date with either of them. I would get drunk, want sex, then call any willing participant I knew; simple as that. I associated alcohol with sex. Both were an escape. Both were required to accompany the other. There was almost no separating the two. I was twenty-eight years old and my reputation had never been something I had considered, and I certainly didn't think I had been important enough for anyone to talk about. It just hadn't occurred to me and I was shocked into reality when my girlfriend, a co-worker, confronted me at work. She asked in a high whisper, "Girl, I heard you dated like three guys that work here. Is that true?" I was floored with embarrassment. I didn't lie. I didn't say anything. That evening, I had some kind of nervous breakdown. I sat there thinking and it occurred to me that while the world had labeled me a whore, I was standing in the middle of me, my history and all of my context with an important life issue to sort out. This was bigger than the world's judgment of me. I slept around and never usually enjoyed it. What the hell was I doing? This was suddenly about me. Sex had felt extremely overrated because I had always been drunk and didn't truly understand what it was supposed to be. I was thoroughly ashamed of myself and couldn't pinpoint why I had done any of it.

After getting home from work that day, I strained to recall my early sexual experiences and for the first part of the evening I could only go back as far as age thirteen when I remembered having some vividly wild sexual fantasies. Something said to me, "You're a whore. You'll never be married." Then as if God himself spoke into my life, I heard or felt something urge me to, "Keep thinking," and I did. Suddenly, I began to remember what happened when I was a young child. Memories that I had forgotten became real again. Visual images suddenly flooded into consciousness. None of them were audible. Alcohol and sex; groups of people, dirty magazines, a cave and a wooden table, a tall slim adult male and other younger children; altogether the images inundated me. It was exhausting. I was astonished that I had lived almost thirty years without thinking about or remembering such cruelty. It occurred to me that I must have had all sorts of delusions regarding my self-worth and disassociations with sex because of it all. The abuse, the lack of protection from my mother, the alcohol, the lack of self-respect and so on; all of it mattered now. Then I remembered as a young child watching The Oprah Winfrey Show. She had some crackpot guest on who attested to having something called a "suppressed memory". As a little black girl from the south, they sounded like a crazy person to me. Fast forward thirty years and there I was figuring this out now? Who knew you could forget traumatic experiences? I was in shock. By the time I put it all together, I was stark naked with wild hair and over forty-eight hours had gone by without my knowing. The way I picked it apart, there were two options at that point. I could either call my mother and curse her out a new asshole or go to church. I decided to go to church.

Religion and superstition aside, just like any child that experiences abuse, I had been conditioned unfairly and during that two-day period and for the first time ever, I came up with a game plan for a problem that I had not realized I had. I needed counseling and got it. What I learned in counseling was that I was living in a perpetual state of vulnerability, especially given all the liquor I consumed daily. I hated myself and felt inferior to the world. The counseling helped almost immediately and in all my excitement and like a complete drunk idiot, I set out to get married. I met my ex-husband, we started a very healthy dating relationship and then suddenly my brother died. I was devastated all over again. My brother David was like my father. He was my protector. Vulnerability was the furthest thing from my mind. All I knew was that in the midst of my grief, here was this gorgeous man looking at me with love in his eyes. It felt good and I went all in for the first time. I fell in love, got married and had two kids. Turn up!

While married and although unhappy, I stopped drinking excessively and devoted my vagina to my husband. After five years, I quit my job and became a stay-at-home mom. In the final summary, although technically he left me, we both admitted that we were miserable and were not connecting on any level, especially sexually. For hell's sake, we had sex twice in 2009 and got pregnant with our second child. *(Really God?)* It was so strange. I had never had a problem getting laid until I got married although to his credit, we just weren't matched on any level and just didn't get each other at all. Once the marriage ended and I thoroughly put it all into perspective I was able to point out that we were indeed both thoroughly vulnerable, each for a different set of reasons. This is why we fell so madly in love with each other. We were both needy as fuck.

By the time that was over, I had jumped out of the frying pan and right into the fire. I was a mess over my failed marriage when I met Greggory; four months later to be exact. I found myself again, falling in love with someone who was not right for me. It made me think of one time hearing my mother say, "You can't fall in love with every man that smiles at'cha." At the time I wanted to punch her. I thought, "Ok fine, I won't fall in love. I'll just have sex!! I've been practicing since I was five years old you bitch!" (I would never talk to my mother like that. I think at my mother like that.) At any rate, I was facing tremendous obstacles; then recently divorced, with two small children; I had no job and was poor. I was in recovery for alcoholism; I was heartbroken, fearful about my daughter who was developing special needs, I was underweight, dehydrated, depressed, drinking too many coca-colas and generally confused as hell. I had no plan and no direction. Thinking about starting a new relationship at that time was like trying to tie up a wild monkey in a hot desert. It was dumb and I lost miserably.

When my player got a hold of me, I must have shined like a Super Nova. I was the absolute *perfect* mark. Looking back, I had never required him to step up to his "A" game because what little attention he gave me was sufficient, given all my damned neediness. Until that point in my life, I had remained either emotionally detached or love addicted; only desiring love in the intervals following a traumatic experience. This time, I had my claws all out and ready to sink right into him. At one point, I pounced onto him! This took some of the slack from my offender in my opinion. It then became apparent that because of my messiness, I could not blame him for the hurt that I was feeling. I too had contributed in great degree to the establishing and continuing of a relationship I knew full well was unhealthy. Realizing this was a crucial stage to my recovery.

Once a vulnerable woman falls in love, her love interest will have no one to compete with. A player knows that once in love, she will pour all of herself into him. There will be no more room in her head for another man. She will feel as if she has found her solution. Being with her player rushes her brain and body with dopamine (our primary "pleasure hormone") which makes her happy; period. How could anyone compete? Once she is hooked, his lack of a sincere interest in her *whole* person begins to leave her hungry for his attention. He only desires a small part of her; her body and devotion and neglects her other interests and needs. For the player, this develops into an organic perk because when he does pinch off a little bit of his time and energy, she is utterly grateful and that feels good to him. Her desperation is what he is attracted to.

For the player, what feels like reasonable victory turns out to be a preying upon the weakened; a kicking of who is down. It is likely this perspective has never occurred to the player and apart from someone explaining it; he may never give this concept consideration. He may continue to prey on the weak for a lifetime whether aware or unaware of his need for vulnerable women.

Some know it and own it. His personality as player is not important. The take away here is to be aware of periods where you may be emotionally compromised. Understand that it is never a good idea to begin a new relationship immediately following a traumatic loss or experience. You are susceptible to emotional danger so following times of distress; make company with people you know and trust.

MASCULINITY

The basic structure of the male ego stems from his need to develop his masculinity. His sense of masculinity coincides with his sense of competence and he is biologically driven to differentiate himself as winner or loser. His culture, his father, his peers and his female relationships have, throughout his lifetime, reinforced his motivation to show the world he can succeed instead of fail. Within every male is a built-in hierarchy and he spends his life gauging where he falls on that scale. He must associate himself with one who either wins or loses at any given stage in his life. The alpha male, chopped full of testosterone, finds his way into the pecking order by making alliances with other alpha males; even doing favors for and imitating them, fully becoming inducted into a rich, male stronghold. His is a natural crowd mentality; especially when bonding with other males. His drive is to prove that he is capable of appealing to others and achieving the figurative upper hand. He must first prove this to himself and then to his social circles. To show the world failure would be opposite to his foremost inspiration in life and is a highly stressful imagination for him to perceive. If they fail at winning in an area, they will choose another avenue to compete. Men are essentially addicted to winning. Winning to him feels like and looks very much like what illicit drugs do to the brain. My grandmother said to me once, "You have to *give* a man a lil' victory sometimes. Pretend you can't open the peanut butter jar every now and again. He needs it." She was right.

Men secure their sense of masculinity with sex. His relationship to sex becomes his barometer for masculinity; therefore, the area of sex is often where a man feels his deepest sense of pain. The issues surrounding his sexuality run the gamut but moreover this is the area that men suffer with the most. Perceived sexual dysfunction is what Psychologists say is of the top reported reasons men seek psychological help. We all know men don't like seeing the doctor; unless it's a "fix my penis" doctor! He is more likely to seek help if he occasionally fails at achieving erection than occasionally having heart palpitations. When the issue of impotence arises, a sexual man goes into panic mode. His fear is that he will not be genuinely and sexually desired and its seeds are in his culture. His sense of masculinity borders around his ability to connect with his world on a sexual level. For some, sitting in front of a computer does the trick. For others, constant illicit sexual relationships are what it takes. At any rate, men chase after a comfortable level of sexual connectivity in order to understand themselves as male. Whatever kind of man he is, his masculinity is in some way married to his relationship with sex.

Authors of an article in The British Journal of Sexual Medicine published in 2011 suggest that "...becoming a man meant establishing oneself as having physical competence, social adeptness and acceptance, and personal power. Esteem was gained through positive regard from male peers and from having girlfriends." His social circles are important to him. He needs both masculine and feminine energy in his life. That's a given but this statement ties another important aspect into what makes a man masculine; that is his need to be physical. He needs his muscles in order to process stress and life in general. In males, muscles and the nervous system are more linked than females. As boys, language and vocabulary are learned partially through his muscles. This "embodied cognition" causes little boys to remain in almost constant motion. They can't seem to sit still for very long because everything they are taking in is linked to their muscles. Moving things, as in himself or a ball for example, will help him process stress, learn, express himself verbally and so on. And of course, as physical, sexual beings, the male roots much of his social and personal identity through his ideas about sex. Physical movement and interactions are important to male humans in a way that women cannot relate. The female requires emotional interactions like talking to process and learn through life. They engage their brains to relieve stress whereas men need to turn theirs off and go have sex or hit the gym; or both. A huge part of his masculinity resides in his ability to prove himself physically.

To win in the sexual arena, he must secure satisfaction by any means necessary. To avoid rejection, he will try any creative maneuver imaginable. Some seek porn exclusively to alleviate any risk of rejection. The player on the other hand will coerce his mark for sex rather than seeking any deeper approval from her. This way, the sex is on his terms and he can control his potential level of rejection. In the game between the player and the mark, it is not his concern whether she accepts his true self. He in fact hides his true self from her. If she rejects his false self, it does not sting as deeply and he can walk away emotionally unscathed. It is his concern however that she become enamored with him for a period of time; sex or no sex. If he hooks her emotionally, it gives him the illusion of acceptance and requires the least amount of his effort and time. Because he is putting on an act, he avoids actually becoming introspective. Ultimately, his intention is to prove to himself that he can capture her mind and body and become sexually desirable. He will use whatever strategy that works, even if it means pretending to be a completely different person.

Masculinity is also what drives him to posture. Before a challenge, male hormones get all up in a bunch and some very instinctive triggers begin to play; namely, Mr. "I'll show *you* whose boss!" When cornered with failure, the male will find an area of dominance to stand on, especially when challenged by his sex partner. In a situation that he can't win, he may pretend not to care. He may also pretend to be angry to divert attention and avoid a conversation. Most men seem to become angry when cornered but according to research, some of this behavior is posturing. Some men posture more astutely than others but masculinity certainly involves masquerading as confident and sometimes pissed. I used to do this when I was drunk at work. If I looked like an angry black woman, no one bothered me. Looking angry helps you hide in plain sight and works damned near every time. Some scientists even believe that a man's beard is designed to hide his facial expressions; specifically fear. Only a rare few have the good judgment to understand when not to be offended by a tough-guy act; namely, wizards and other magical people.

LOVE

Scientists, philosophers and psychologists have through the years attempted to define *love*. Until recent neuroimaging capabilities, the search for understanding the neural origins of love remained theoretical. Thanks to the availability of functional MRI machines, studies of neurotransmitters, more specifically the dopaminergic system, it is possible to observe that love and sexuality live deep in the brain's limbic system and is related with the circuits that process reward, desire and pleasure. Scientists have been able to observe the brain while it is falling in love, falling out of love and sustained in life-long, loved filled marriages. As each phase and form of love is distinct, so are their neurological profiles.

Unconditional love is a deep concept that I believe begins to make sense to people after having children. It is difficult to explain the new level of general human tolerance, forgiveness and explicitly unconditional love you feel and extend to your own offspring. Not to say one can't discover these concepts in other ways, only that my children are what taught me. At the end of the day, true love is a choice. By definition "unconditional" means "not subject to the state of something, especially with regard to its appearance, quality, or working order" (Oxford Dictionaries); therefore, unconditional love means choosing to continually act in another's benefit despite who they are, what they look like, how far they get ahead in life or whether they are in any way broken. I'd say that's much different than choosing to love someone *only* when they behave. A crazy person can do that. You should love people even when they misbehave otherwise it's kind of like declaring, "I only feed my kids when they make good grades," or more appropriately realizing that, "He only treats me nice when he wants some head." Do the math. Acting in a loving manner towards someone *only* when they do what you want doesn't amount to loving or caring for them. Actually, it amounts to using them for convenience.

"IN LOVE"

When someone is falling into romantic love, specific regions of the limbic system light up with activity, right around where your brain connects to your spinal cord. This activity triggers sexual and emotional circuits that affect the body in a ton of interesting ways, even intensifying a person's sense of smell. When these areas activate, the brain triggers hormones that change the smell of your sweat so it emits a special recipe of chemicals called pheromones. Inside the nose, their partner's *nasal*alae (nasal passages) will process the scent of these pheromones in a way that only the brain can. You certainly can't sniff the air and detect that your lover is about a block away but your brain can. (Well maybe not a whole city block but the possibility also hasn't been disproved.) If they are in love, a couple's brains are literally reacting to the other's pheromones and in essence, their brains are working in unison towards a very primal mating instinct which results in levels of dopamine that make them feel like they can read each other's minds. It feels like euphoria. Let's not set aside that it is the sudden rush of dopamine during orgasm that creates a similar euphoric feeling. Even if one of them is lying about being in love, the other's brain will still detect enough of the lusty pheromones which will promote the perception that the love they feel is mutual. Incidentally, if their brains were both analyzed on an fMRI, it would be apparent which one of them is pretending.

"Out Of Love"

Unfortunately, this "falling in love" phenomenon is short-lived. If the couple remain together for any considerable amount of time, their blissfulness will eventually wane as the limbic system ceases to activate at the same levels as before. This usually happens somewhere within the range of one and a half to two years. At this stage, the couple may feel like the relationship has gone sour. What they do not realize is that this seemingly "falling out of love" feeling is a natural neurological progression of emotive response. It is a leveling back down to normal. The same circuits in the limbic system are no longer lighting up and dopamine is not hot-triggered anymore when you gaze into your lover's eyes. Suddenly, you require more stimulation to generate that same euphoric feeling. Dopamine acts as a cortisol suppressant so when his brain is falling in love, her naivety will not create the same stress response that it will a couple years down the road when the same high levels of dopamine are not present. Consequently, the naivety that attracted him to her at first has become annoying. Similarly, she used to think it was cute when he forgot where he parked. Not so much anymore. Once the infatuation is over, suddenly the stress is surviving all the way to her frontal lobe every time she has to help him find the damned car. Once the temporary euphoria ends, the real work of love and relationships begins.

"Choosing Love"

Once the infatuation phase is over and if the couple remains together, the perception of love becomes something different. It becomes a clear choice. Falling in love is very sex-linked and can feel automatic once the phenomenon takes hold. Staying in love is what takes the real work. I've heard it said before that love is a verb and I agree. Love is the effort I make when I'm ill with the flu and get up at 3:00 AM anyway to care for my sick children. Love is holding back my frustration to patiently teach. Love is calling someone to remind them that I'm concerned about what they are concerned about. Love is making sure to leave a positive impression on someone else's life. Love is being selfless, slow to anger, generous, heartfelt, caring and engaging in a giving and taking of emotions. The player wants absolutely nothing to do with such debauchery. The cold truth is he is not intending to love anything or anyone. He is simply out to gain conveniences. The player is choosing not to love. Consider that when it comes to his romantic relationships, 50% of his objective is to output the least amount of effort. No matter how he intends to use his mark, he wants to find the shortest, easiest route. His goal is to push her to her limit emotionally and get as close to that *nose-wide-open* girlfriend experience as possible; no matter what he feels or doesn't feel about her. The remaining 50% of his objective is purely sexual. Nowhere is there room for love in his strategy.

Love is also not a feeling. It is pure choice of acting out towards another's benefit. Feelings come and go like the seasons and if we were to be led by them, we'd fail at everything because emotional feelings are fleeting and unstable. Emotions are to be controlled and endured while we manage our tangible lives. You don't feel like going to work but you do it anyway. Sometimes you don't feel like doing any damned thing for anybody but you do everything anyway. Sometimes you feel like giving up on people but you don't. Love requires that you keep wishing them well. Love is not a promise nor is it an exchange. It is a one-way choice that says, "I will mean well for you no matter what you do."

Love is definitely a verb and therefore it is apparent. If Jane runs in the sand, Jane leaves footprints. The actions of another's love should be evident. If you are in love with someone but feel you are constantly seeking proof and reassurance of their feelings for you, it may be time to reconsider. The evidence may not be there and you may be in a situation where your heart is being toyed with. Although tempting, to imagine in your fantasy that someone loves you is unwise and changes your biology. Don't do it.

SCIENCE IS KEY

On a very general note, understanding behavior and emotion requires an understanding of science. We are biological creatures that have been scientifically studied, poked at and experimented on; albeit not all have been ethical practices – God forbid the horrendously unethical and

downright cruel direction science went in during the 19th century –
nonetheless, if you dig a little, you'll discover amazing scientific
advancements that have allowed us to somewhat make sense of humanity.
We can either choose to guess why we do and feel or we can learn the
science behind it. After which we can then make an educated assessment
about the world around us and the relationships we engage in. Science is
important. Guesswork is futile.

It is unfortunate that the history of psychology has excluded its education
to the general public. Most of us have bought in to the idea that medical
science is too complicated and only elite professionals need comprehend
such important matters. Bullshit. We, the general public, have left ourselves
unaware, unsuspecting and unprotected. We wait until something goes
wrong to see a doctor – if we don't die first. We have little to no knowledge
of the process, history and implications of scientific research, how it has
evolved world ideologies, politics and the overall survival of the earth and
human race. This means we have no idea how to prevent mental and
physical health problems because we haven't the slightest clue how or why
we become ill. Once we get hurt, we seek help to fix a problem that in most
cases could have been prevented with a sound education and application of
that education; in other words, knowledge.

"Don't smoke cigarettes, eat your vegetables and brush your teeth," are
some of the basic strategies we understand are important to physical health
but what about our minds? What about understanding how you can
preserve or destroy healthy behaviors? Therefore, can understanding
human behavior help us avoid making kneejerk love decisions that lead to

heartache? Of course it can. Our psychology; that is our way of thinking, is not some continuum of random notions, toggling between loosing and gaining control. When it is convenient, we assume that we can't control our thoughts and behaviors. Other times, we pride ourselves with possessing great control over both. Well... which one is it?

We operate by use of both voluntary and involuntary actions derived from our bodies and minds. We have reflexes we cannot control and yet, many times we have some power to control them. If your Thanksgiving turkey is ready to come out of the oven and halfway from the oven to the counter, you discover there is a hole in your oven mitt, you will feel intense pain in your palm. Your autonomic nervous system (which handles your *involuntary* actions) will trigger your body to open both hands and let go of the turkey. This is a reflex. The trouble is you can't ruin Thanksgiving so you resist. This means your somatic nervous system (which handles your *voluntary* actions) will trigger your muscles to move quickly, bouncing the turkey like a hot potato and tossing it safely on the closest flat surface. The same thing applies to the individual that suffers from mental panic attacks. The anxiety response is involuntary as their brain signals inappropriate fear. This person must apply somatic control over their emotions and voluntarily decide against fear. They must find a way that calms them until the attack is over by applying strategies like slow, deep breathing or mental visualizing. Using these strategies, they can actually adjust the chemicals in their brains back to normal faster.

Our physical and mental selves work unanimously so just as you have principal control over your physical body, you also are Captain over the chemicals floating around in your brain. The danger is that when you are hurt emotionally, feelings can become the main event. While hurt, it is easy to neglect tending to the chemicals and circumstances that are causing the pain. The take away here is that you have more mind control than you think and if you thought otherwise, it is only because you need a little basic training in science. In this pursuit to understand our codependent relationships, it is vital that we discover appropriate psychology.

Why should it matter at all when people are discordant with our sexual and emotional desires? After all, we get to choose who enters and exits our lives. Some folks will fit, some won't. The burden is on us to decide who gets to stay within our life space and further, on what conditions. Psychology can help us navigate through and around people, personalities and social situations. This section is to help you understand the field that we're playing on here is the science of human nature. We're not debating whether the nature of males or females is better or worse or whether players or marks have some moral or emotional deficit. The idea is that you come to a basic understanding of where you ended up so you can get through it without a scratch. Trying to navigate through heartbreak unaware is like kicking a dead horse up a hill. You won't succeed without a strategy. You need tools and help from others. Guesswork in the realm of heartbreak will leave you wrangled and exhausted so from a psychological standpoint and in the famous words of the greatest American hero, "knowing is half the battle." [G.I. Joe, circa 1982]

CHAPTER 2 | THE OBJECT OF THE GAME

"**play-er** (ˈplāər/) *noun: player; plural noun: players* – a person taking

part in a sport or game." ~ *Google Definition 2018*

In relationships, there are all types of "players" and many interpret this label loosely. In most circles it is fashionable to be the player or a more glamorous term; *the womanizer*. In many ways, especially in film, the player is esteemed as the good guy or at least normal. He is forever handsome, charming, the perfect lover and of course he always gets the girl. Interestingly, players are socially accepted and their female counterparts, typically referred to as *sluts* or *whores*, are continually rejected in society. The irony is that the whore is providing free, consensual sex to men who treat her with very little regard and when she disappears, typically she's not leaving an emotionally scarred partner behind. The player, on the other hand, provides sex for an emotional price, is treated with a kingly regard and leaves a glut of emotional wreckage in his wake.

To clarify the scope of *"the complete player"*, let us first define what it is not so you do not confuse your particular situation. Let us be clear; the complete player is the extreme womanizer. He is not just the man who has sex with a lot of women. He is not the man who has multiple one-night stands and he is not the man who desires to pursue women only for sex without marriage. The complete player encompasses all of the above but the distinguishing characteristic of the player is his unique *give and take* strategy. He takes by requiring his mark's full sexual and emotional cooperation. What he gives, however, is his bare minimum. Get the most while giving as little as possible. This is the game. To achieve this, he must play on a woman's love triggers. He knows that if he can get her to fall in love, she will cooperate out of desperation. Some women will hang on forever, others will not. His game never stops and is fueled by a deep and dominant need to prove to himself that he is desirable.

In this context, the object of the game is to manipulate another's emotional attachment for personal gain. Therefore, the player *is* the man who is not forthright about his intentions or lack thereof. He is the man that does not give a woman transparency or the choice of a no strings attached relationship. On the contrary, he wants the strings and pretends to be emotionally available; creating a completely new personality that effectively lures women into his control. The player tends to take whole emotional control of the relationship and the other person involved, leaving the mark feeling inferior, unsatisfied and unable to express her emotions at all. His game is simple and has two parts. First, he baits and then he switches. He leads her on until she shows signs of strong feelings then disengages to see how long she hangs around. If she has fallen into that just right configuration of dysfunction and love, it will take her ages to disappear and the skillful player can enjoy her benefits for a potential lifetime.

It is also important to establish that the game we are referring to is not a fair one. To the player, it is a numbers game that is played solo. It is not a match set. He is the only participant. To him, she is not an opponent. She is a task; a goal, and she remains like an unsuspecting deer, caught in headlights, only aware of danger after is it too late. By the time she catches on, she is hit and he is gone. To the mark, it is a love game that is being played by two hearts, his and hers. Hers however, is the only game that can be lost. His is won by numbers so each task, even if unsuccessful, does not compute with ultimate failure and simply creates motivation to acquire more numbers. It does not matter to him whether he acquires sex. If a mark happens to leave him before sex happens, there is no loss. He simply does not win that one.

It is like children playing dodge ball. The player is the one throwing the ball. If he misses, he simply tries again; increasing his chances of hitting someone on each attempt. The moment they are hit, the participants in the middle are out of the game. They lose while the thrower keeps on throwing; impervious to the participants he's already conquered. His focus is on the few that are left standing in the middle. As long as he keeps throwing, he wins. Once he's whittled down his partakers to the last woman standing and there is no one else to throw at, she is his prize; his trophy. The only way the player loses is if he finds himself old, alone and unable to connect with a suitable mate. There is no end game. As with children, there is just playtime.

It is yet more important to point out an ironic fact that mutually, both the player and the mark have an ulterior motive to conquer each other. Both want to acquire the other's body and mind. The difference lies in the degrees to which each wants to conquer. Both want to conquer on their own terms for a specified scope of time; his vision being indefinite while hers is clearly long-term. To him, there is no significance to whether he remains involved for a few minutes or a lifetime. To her, there is a great significance to the time she spends building a long-term sexual and emotional partnership. The expectation is that each party will devote certain attentions to each other. The player wants *the illusion* of love without the work that love requires while the mark strives for *the full experience* of love; with all its requirements and at a bare minimum sex, caring attention, forgiveness and consideration. If her love interest is a player, she will not experience any illusion of loving behaviors. The reality is that only the player can achieve his goal. The mark, on the other hand, will fail in her endeavors no matter where she slates her standards.

For the mark, finding the comfort that a man loves her usually starts in her fantasy. Her vision of love becomes the expectation that she places on her love interest so she fantasies without restraint. When she realizes she has invested too much emotionally, she places up her guards, begins asking questions or otherwise shows her hurt feelings. Subsequently to the player, she then becomes less convenient and therefore less interesting. This is a very odd parallel. Initially, he commissions her love and later rejects it. The mark initially craves feelings of love until she despises them. The difference is, she leaves with a broken heart and he is left unharmed.

To the unsuspecting female, detecting her love emotion is being toyed with can be confusing, frustrating and sometimes, without psychic powers, impossible. Eventually, if she manages to figure him out, it is at that stage when a woman may make the difficult step to severe the relationship. If she can muster the strength to leave, what follows is a stage wherein one text from him can cause a whirlwind of confusion. It feels hurtful when her player makes any attempt at contacting her. It stings because it causes her brain to fire an absolute hot mess, bittersweet chemical cocktail that feels good, bad and ugly all at the same time. After each conversation she has to fight off old, unhealthy feelings that impede her healing. She may spend countless hours trying to understand what happened to *him* before she even considers what actually happened to *her*. She'll wonder whether he had feelings at one point that went away or whether he ever had them at all. Eventually she may find herself shuffling through her memories, assessing a timeline of her feelings against her player's actions. The acquiescent woman may blame her own behavior for having run him off but if she is astute, she will see that there two clear stages of the game; The Baiting Act and The Disappearing Act.

THE BAITING ACT

For the player, the initial choice of his mark is not complicated. He simply chooses anyone that is receptive to his advances. He's looking for a coy smile instead of a frown or any obvious sign that a woman is sexually interested. Eye contact is his first line of attack so there is nothing special about how he chooses his mark other than the fact that she is looking at him. His game becomes valid by the simple act of choosing her; simultaneously he is deciding between a challenge and the impossible. If he does not choose her, it simply means he believes she is not interested and therefore impossible to win. If he chooses her, he simply thinks he has a chance at sex. He is not thinking anything else through. It makes no difference what her intellectual, social-economic or otherwise status is; he simply chooses her because she is there and seems willing to participate.

Once a player has marked a woman, he knows his best tool at baiting is waiting. He waits patiently for sex no matter how long it takes and although he may fail; his goal is not to be the first to initiate. At his core, he plays this game because he needs reassurance that he is masculine. He needs to feel desired and waiting causes her desire to increase. Finally, her initiation of sex proves his ego so he does not chase and lets her seek him out; always making sure to be as available as possible. This means in the beginning, although he may not initiate conversation, he will almost always reply or call back quickly. This feels like loving attention to some women. Some men pursue sex vigorously which to a woman can seem unoriginal and desperate; not to mention creepy. It can turn a woman off from a man very suddenly. The contrast is a man who can wait for sex. For women, this trait symbolizes desirability in a life-mate. With the player, however, it may mean he's simply having difficulty managing contact with the women in his life. It is much easier to wait until they each initiate contact with him. If he continually sows his seeds; always marking new prospects; as they mature, he can enjoy a year-round harvest with very little effort.

He has learned that not pursuing her sexually will build her trust more quickly. When a woman is alone in a room with a man she is attracted to for any considerable amount of time, she expects him to make some kind of move on her and readies herself. She waits for a flirtatious wink or a kiss and even the old "pop it out" routine. She expects one of three scenarios; 1) to accept his advances, 2) to defer his pursuit to a more appropriate time or 3) to reject him altogether. If he doesn't try, she may assume that he was displaying a kind of respect for her. The waiting feels like respect to some women because it is not what she is used to. If a woman is suffering under some inferiority complex, alcoholism, drug addiction or some otherwise disease of the mind, this waiting stage will be her hook, line and sinker. Players therefore have ample success when they encounter women fresh off of some life trauma or otherwise mentally compromised. For these women, present company included, this waiting is enough to prove his affection. His lack of sexual pursuit is misinterpreted as evidence of patience. It is really the laziest of strategies and requires less work. A few meals, a concert and a few nights of cuddling then disengage interest. It's enough to send any vulnerable woman reeling for more attention.

My player did not make the initial sexual advances. He waited for me to feel comfortable enough to make the first move which occurred after talking, spooning, kissing and cuddling in my bedroom every other weekend or so for four months. I trusted him because he listened to me. I believed his interests mirrored mine and it aroused me something awful. I couldn't get him off my mind and thought about his skin, scent, voice and face constantly. He was an incredible distraction to all the post-divorce difficulty I was going through. I was sufficiently baited into everything about him. I was hooked and at the time, couldn't put my finger on why he felt like a drug addiction.

At this early stage in male attraction, no feelings are involved, and only strategies are at play. Whether he's patiently waiting for sex because he doesn't have the nerve or whether he is being decisive, she is becoming attached. This is where the mark begins to feel the phenomenon of love while her player remains tactical. At this stage and going forward, her reactions will determine how her player strategizes for sex. If his challenge becomes too easy, he minimizes his strategy. If she presents a reasonable test, he increases it. If she cues in and shuts him down, he does an about-face and throws the dodge ball at someone else.

THE DISAPPEARING ACT

The moment a mark divulges to her player she feels deeply for him, the ice suddenly thins and he may take a step backwards; immediately becoming less available, sometimes disappearing from her life altogether. During the days when she's looking for him, she develops a natural insecurity that fuels her obsession. At this stage, it has not occurred to her that he may have been dishonest in his behaviors, words or body language. If she is in love, she expected that he also experienced a buildup of emotional feelings similar to the ones she developed. It is exacerbating to try and understand what happened to someone else's feelings. In fact, it is downright impossible and to engage in such guesswork is torture. When a man disappears during this stage, it can leave a woman confused and desperate. Her brain is not equipped to process this type of emotional shock and goes into a somewhat of a withdrawal from the readily amounts of adrenaline, dopamine and oxytocin he has been causing to flow. This creates a chemical imbalance in her brain which has an acute effect on the rest of her body.

The term "love sick" has a very scientific root and her behavior may begin to bend towards erratic. This causes him to move even further away from her. The player will exhaust every length to avoid engaging in the subject of feelings. If directly confronted, he will miraculously find an exit. Ultimately, if she corners him, rather than divulge the truth, he will stall with familiar words and then disappear. "I'll call you right back," is likely the most widely used strategy, short of an abrupt "I don't need this right now," and then click to a dial tone. (For the younger generation, a "dial tone" is a sound that happens when you hang up an analog telephone.) The challenge has become too difficult and the game is now over. He will either cut her off completely if she has proven too dramatic or, if she is not too temperamental, he will leave a "forever door" open for her should she ever lose strength and seek him out.

Typically, when a man engages a woman romantically, then suddenly disengages, it means he may be experiencing love feelings. Feelings of love are terrifying to men so often they will step away from their love object to regroup and protect themselves emotionally. This is very common with men. They run and yet if these feelings are genuine, these men eventually come back to pursue the women they love. In the case of the player however, since he is avoiding love feelings at all cost, his disengagement means he's done putting in the work on his mark. He moves on and sometimes, if he is fortunate, his most desperate marks conveniently follow.

THE MARK

The choice to pursue a selected mark is fairly straight forward for the player. He's looking for beauty and moreover she must be submissive and weakened. If he were forced to forego one of these it would be beauty. She *must* be vulnerable, which is the sum of the remaining two requirements; submission and weakness. He is looking for someone who is desperate enough to play along – a woman who shows signs of emotional turmoil or extenuating circumstances like a recent breakup, loss or a general broken spirit. Intelligence is not a requirement in his selection; in fact, it could be a deterrent. Her intelligence may intrigue him in the beginning, but if she continues to tolerate his ill behaviors, her qualities of submission and weakness will overshadow her intelligence and beauty. However, if he is lucky enough to happen upon a beautiful, intelligent women who is submissive and weak, he will consider it an added layer to his challenges; an enticement to the chase.

Her weakness will either be emotional, financial or both and he will prey on whatever weakness he can tend to. To feed her emotional dependencies, he will simply listen to her and remember what she says because his experiences have taught him that this level of attention, albeit fairly easy to pull off, will almost guarantee that his mark fall for him. Her brain is designed to trigger the perfect cocktail of the "love producing" brain chemicals, oxytocin and dopamine when verbally connecting with her love interest. To feed her financial dependencies, if he is financially secure enough, he will help only if asked. He needs her to need him. If he is financially able, a player can on some levels and for a duration of time, satisfy both his mark's emotional and financial needs with very little effort.

He needs to merely remember what she says and give her money. In her emotional state, this will feel like he cares.

He need not tend to her intellect or beauty and if left unattended, she will become obsessed with appealing to him in these areas, showing off to him whenever possible. She may share her accomplishments, text random dirty pictures of herself or even fantasize about him acting in a caring way towards her. She'll remain in a sort of "limbo" trying to progress mutual feelings in the relationship to no avail. He is aware that he no longer has to work for her love. Her intellect and talent therefore become a mere perk; an area of amusement for him. No amount of showing off will conjure his respect for her. From the player's vantage, the mark has been placed securely in a love-hungry category of women that don't require much work. Eventually, his original challenge will be met and no unusual efforts are required to maintain her attention. For the player, the relationship becomes one of convenience and is more than likely, one of many.

In those first few soft conversations between the mark and her player; late at night on the phone lying flat in bed, it is important that he ask her deep intimate details about her life experiences. Many women are eager to share and he is aware his listening makes her feel more connected. For him, it is merely a gathering of information. In my case, within a few days after our first kiss, I divulged to my player that I had been sexually raped from the ages of five to seven; that I was a recovering alcoholic with about thirty days of sobriety and that when I was ten years old my father went to prison for killing an infant. To him it must have been crystal clear. I was the perfectly ripe for the marking. Finally, I had answered the question, "Why me?"

Up until my point of discovery, I could not understand why he had not just picked someone easier than me but in truth, it is not easy sex the player is after. The mark is a challenge. She is the goal in the sport of seduction. Seducing a woman that is likely to remain emotionally detached doesn't present the challenge he desires. Marking an emotionally detached woman would be equivalent to playing basketball with the net at half height. Lowering the stakes makes for a less interesting game while men seek self-challenge. He wants to prove to himself that he can capture the heart of a woman. Illicit sex, however, is a low stakes game that is played regularly and casually during periods when his "A" game is not producing its desired results. He will elect his favorite drunk whore or prostitute when schedules cannot coincide. For the player who has a myriad of women to choose from, his favorite mark will be his first choice because her emotionally devoted sex is sometimes more pleasurable than easy sex.

At any rate, I came in hot and full of emotion. I was like a budding ivy plant, ready to attach to whatever surface I could cling to. There was nothing detached about me this time. I was fresh off divorce; love starved, newly sober clinging to my Alcoholics Anonymous family and didn't know what the hell to think about anything. I was the perfect catch for a player. Once I understood why he chose me, it laid the groundwork for the healing that I desperately needed and the forgiveness that was to come. All told, I realized that there was nothing so special about me. I had just happened to cross his path and was emotionally injured enough to accommodate whatever he dished out. He essentially had me at "hello" and really didn't need to do much. Admittedly, I was extremely attracted to him and made a clear decision to be receptive to any of his sexual advances. I was ready. As a follow up, the way he used his body language, words and money worked like a charm. He was kind and thoughtful at first and did not pursue sex. Hook, line and sinker; I was in love because I thought he truly cared about me and I moved towards him as fast as I could.

Body Language

In the book *The Male Brain*, Dr. Louann Brizendine explains *"contact readiness cues"* as a term used to describe communicative triggers to the brain detected through the observance of non-verbal body language and movement. In other words, fMRI scans can reveal what the brain does when it picks up body language from others. Flirting is a game of contact readiness and men that do it well become the most dangerous players. If the player can effectively read and deliver non-verbal body language, he can detect all the "tells" that a woman is ready for or thinking about sex or whether she feels insecure, fearful or intrigued. He can then return body language that she will accept. The player is an actor. Mine was and is a talented performance artist.

Women that can read contact readiness cues become susceptible targets if the complete player knows how to fake his body language. If he is an expert player, he leans in when speaking to her, never crosses his arms and forces a confidently relaxed frame. He stares into her eyes as she talks, remains quiet and waits for her to look away first. This makes her feel as if he is looking straight into her soul. She believes that even if he is not seeing through her, he definitely wants to. To her brain, intense eye contact feels like deep human connection and causes a sincere interest in dropping emotional guards. This "melting point" varies from woman to woman. Generally, the more dysfunctional she is, the quicker she melts. The typical female brain cannot detect insincerity and commences to fire its required dose of dopamine and oxytocin when connecting with other humans. This means her feelings may grow deeper with each stare. Respectively, the player may cease flirting once he detects his mark is securely baited; that is, after she is experiencing feelings of love. If she chooses to continue seeing him, he no longer needs to exert the energy to flirt. If she becomes as desperate as he hopes, she will do enough flirting for the both of them.

If she allows him to become sexually physical with her, the player fully understands his first impression must be impressive because it will likely be the only full physical effort he will ever yield out to her. His only requirement is that once or twice, he attend to her every inch and sexual need. Once this requirement is met, he may disengage in his efforts to please her altogether. It is important, however that their first sexual encounters be momentous for her so he uses every trick and position he knows. He must take control of the pleasure principle and bait her with sexual body language. If he knows she's falling in love, he is aware that he is fulfilling her dream; one she has pictured in her fantasies many times. The first few times in bed with a man are momentous for the female if she cares about him so he does his best to mimic passion. He kisses her, caresses her and attends to her entire body. He makes love to her. He is trying to take full control of her fantasy life. The result of his fleeting efforts will be her sexual loyalty, even after he develops as a selfish lover; rarely if ever directly tending to her pleasure.

His experiences (not his extensive research in neuroscience) have taught him sound lines of attack. The player puts forth very little effort after the initial hard work involved in hooking a mark emotionally and during this stage, his expertise is a learned behavior that has come about organically. While he may not be aware of the science behind why his strategies work, he fully understands their results. He has learned that staring at a woman intently while she shares a personal story makes her fidget and smile and he pockets that strategy, applying it the next time with great success. Once she is in love, his battles are won and he no longer bothers making eye contact at all; especially during sex. Initially, his mark may feel and even be fulfilled sexually and emotionally. Very soon after, he ceases his efforts in and out of bed.

WORDS

The player's most valuable tool is his words. Lie or truth, what comes out of his mouth is what a mark in love will hold tight to. There are a myriad of creative ways words can be used to persuade and insight. We all respond in some way to compliments, outright lies, deep honest sharing, scolding and soft and harsh tones. All of what a man says and how he says it has a deep impact on a woman as she tries to put together a cohesive picture of his character. If he is clever, he can be most persuasive by using words.

The most impressive and memorable word strategy my player employed was causing me to believe he told his mother about me within days of our romantic involvement. We had our first kiss just the previous night and he was due to arrive at my apartment late morning to help me run an errand. I was excited to see him and went outside all the way to the sidewalk to greet him. After embracing, I escorted him up my driveway when I noticed he was still talking into his earphones mid-conversation with someone. I walked a few feet ahead of him, listening of course, and heard him almost sing, "...at *Samantha's* house." I turned, batted my eyes and smiled at him. He smiled back. Surely, he knew what I was thinking. "He said my name! This guy must really like me," I gloated to myself. Once inside, he sat down and quickly ended the conversation to this mysterious person by saying, "I love you. Bye". Amidst all my excitement and as casually as I could, I asked him who he had been on the phone with. Of course I did. He had said my name which gave me the right. After a fleeting pause and with a smile, he boasted, "My mama." It's doubtful he was talking to anyone. It was brilliant.

To the player, his elegant words and witty responses are lines and just as a theater actor rehearses his dialog then uses them on cue, the player uses the same words again and again. They are experiments in his research ground as he collects his best "go to" retorts. Eventually, even without his knowing, he will develop an "A-list" of lines that work every time. They become almost reflexive applied to all his verbal interactions in person and on the phone; each tainted with false affections in the form of pet names, goodnight texts and polite yet generic praises. To her, they are an accumulation of evidences that he has feelings for her. For him, these are unrelated events that are simply on repeat.

My player used to cleverly flirt by calling me a pervert. The first time he used it, I had invited him to an event via a text message. He replied his answer as, "Pervert!" I took it as a joke because it was. It was the first time anyone had called me a pervert for such a minor offense. I found it cute, funny and intriguing. Having had a plutonic relationship for a year, this tactic suddenly reintroduced him as a sexual being and I'm certain he carefully observed how I would respond. It was likely an experiment that he used often. This particular word is a fashionable choice because it is playful, sexual and is an excellent gauge for what temperature she will be in terms of her boundaries. I played into the humor and replied, "How'd u know?" Subsequently, he showed up at my event the following night smelling wonderful and looking amazing which became the moment when the dynamic of our relationship shifted to romantic. It was the 6th of September. We had been barely fringing around the "friend zone" and that night, we both displayed a mutual sexual interest. Suddenly, we were hardcore flirting. All because of a one word text message: "Pervert!" It was exhilarating and also brilliant.

Once the ice was broken, he began complimenting me, and I him. He complimented my face, my art, my poems, my writing ability, my insights; everything I displayed, he seemed to love and it meant everything to me because I was desperate for attention. At the time, I was coming out of a failed marriage that had been almost void of compliments. Throughout what felt like an almost eight-year prison sentence, I felt sexually undesired for a set of reasons that I will keep to myself for the sake of privacy. For a woman to loosen her heart to a man she needs to feel paid attention to.

She believes that if a man loves her, he will study her. To her, the proof lies in his compliments. If she changes her hair and he notices, she feels connected to him. My player seemed to notice me and he praised everything I showed him.

If you'll remember another very important word tactic is proving to the mark that he remembers what she says. He proves this by retelling her stories back to her. To master this, he only needs to listen to her and remember key details about her likes and dislikes. She may mention in casual conversation that she's not a huge fan of vanilla ice cream. Three months later, if she mentions vanilla, he can say, "But you hate vanilla." When a man recalls a woman's personal experiences or opinions in conversation, even if he gets it a little wrong, she is pleasantly surprised thinking, "I can't believe he remembered!" It is uncommon for men to recall small personal details like the color clothing she wore, that she had a doctor's appointment last week or further, that she dislikes vanilla ice cream. Therefore, it shocks her, sets a man apart as different and is captivating for the female. At her core, she wants to be listened to.

On the other hand, if a mark complains that her player forgot her birthday, for example, he may alter his strategy and diligently begin calling all his marks on their birthdays. This is merely to prevent this undesirable confrontation from reoccurring, just as a football quarterback understands he must take a few steps backwards after the ball is hiked every time with no exceptions. He is strategically and methodically moving out of harm's way. Based on what he has learned, a player knows it's best to be proactive and "Happy Birthday" is a phrase he can easily use to keep face. If he sets a calendar reminder on his phone and calls them all between 12:01 and 12:30 am on their birthdays, he not only reduces his chances of encountering a conflict, he realizes that although not exactly dishonest, he is depicting a deeper connection to her. For him, this conveniently and metaphorically kills two birds with one stone by avoiding conflict and advancing his objective. Creating verbal scripts and social practices this way can become an organic system for him; a way of life.

MONEY

Of all the manipulative tactics, this one was for me, was the most penetrating. It required my deepest emotional and physical attention throughout my relationship and continued to a period of time after its end and until I was able to completely pull myself up to financial independence. In short, during our relationship I was poor and he was rich. Quite frankly, this complicated things. I loved him and yet as far as I could determine, he esteemed me as high as a hooker. This disturbing concept of being labeled a hooker reared its ugly head every time I found myself in financial straits, forced to ask for his help; typically, about every two or three months and in amounts between $250 and $2000. This amounted to my emotional turmoil because I needed his help as equally as I detested it. Before too long, after his affections for me whittled down to none, the only evidence of our relationship was threaded by exchanges of money and sex. Eventually, there was nothing else; no more dates, no more cuddling and no more intimacy.

I knew he was always willing to assist me if I needed money but because of how it felt to ask for it, I only asked when it was dire. I waited until I received disconnection notices in the mail or until I was down to the one knee with no other option left praying to whatever god that would listen and damned near at a mental psychosis before drudging up the nerve to call and beg. (To me, it felt like begging.) I owned and ran a small house cleaning business in Los Angeles yet still I couldn't manage to get past a few months without needing his money. Yuk!

My fledgling company was also my first business, so it was full of growth challenges and I wasn't making enough to get by. Gradually I developed an indifference to crucial financial challenges simply because I knew I could get $1000 when I needed it. This complicated things even further as I approached my third year of business having grown in infrastructure while horribly failing in growth of revenue. I had spent countless hours pulling overnighters configuring my own databases, creating automated systems that could manage hundreds of staff and thousands of customers with a few clicks of the mouse. I never hired a programmer or technician and saved thousands of dollars doing it all myself. Even more impressive was that I spent virtually nothing to start up and built a fine-tuned, well-oiled machine within a year. I felt like one smart ass. The business model was sound and my plan seemed to be working; that is, if I could figure out how to budget any amount to hiring people. I didn't have enough workers on the ground. Without capital to invest in staffing, I was stuck with a fluctuation between 3 to 10 core staff; not enough to cover my bills and pay them all on time.

I was cancelling some 300 cleaning appointments a month. Money was literally slipping through my fingers. I needed to invest in staffing but had been neglecting the responsibility because I knew it would cost an additional $400 a month to hire enough employees to keep up with the demand. I kept thinking, "That's like an extra car payment! I don't have an extra $400 this month; maybe next month business will increase and I'll have it." It had not occurred to me that I was shooting myself in the foot. By not investing the money, even though I didn't have it, I was blocking any chance at increasing the number of my staff, period. It was actually ridiculous. It also hadn't occurred to me that I had become dependent on someone else's money simply because it was readily available whenever I asked. Eventually, when I ended my relationship with him, I had no choice but to take financial risks. Suddenly, the deciding that his help was no longer available caused every money decision to become a risk, including buying groceries. I had to take $400 from my rent to pay an online staffing site or bust. I was forced to step outside of fear. The moment I made that decision to borrow from my rent, it occurred to me that I had been misplacing my priorities all along.

Good sense would have told me to take the risk and invest in staffing ages ago. Instead, I had depended on my player being there to pull me out of trouble; just in case. It was backwards. I wasn't his responsibility. I had to move away from using him to fill the holes to a place where I could proactively prevent holes from forming. While I had his help, there was never any full culmination of urgency, because I had an ever-present lingering solution; always there; just in case. His availability and willingness to give me money took the urgency out of all my financial plans; its boundaries being progressive that I cannot recall the exact moment the shift occurred. Perhaps it was somewhere along that first year when I toiled for days before asking him for $500. He gave me $1000. It was my first time ever asking him for money and I was shocked, shocked I tell you, that it went so easily.

Because he was rich as hell, he consistently gave me a percentage more than I asked for; usually about 30% to 50% more and sometimes double. If I needed $800, he would transfer $1500 into my bank account. If I asked for $2000, I would get $2500. In my translations, this meant he cared about me. In reality, it likely meant nothing. Wealthy men use their money for sex, either to attain it blatantly with a prostitute or by indirect affiliation, enjoying the benefit that loads of women flock to men with money. Further, poor women need it. In fact, what comes with a rich man's feverish work ethic is an underlying motivation that equates the amount of money he has with the frequency of his sexual encounters. He makes more money so he can get more sex. This is no mystery. There was nothing special about the help he gave me. Through a friend, there was only one other woman I learned about who was also a poor single mother and like me an entertainer among other similarities in fact, barring our skin tone, we almost matched exactly. Rumor had it, "he gave her a thousand dollars twice," and upon hearing that, I remembered having never felt so un-special.

Women are attracted to prestige for many reasons. Some are downright bold about seeking money and never love. Most women however, are generally attracted to a provider figure because he is the one that stands out from the masses. He is accomplished, secure, determined and ambitious; a likely candidate as her protector and lover. She is designed as the "gatherer" and her mate as the "hunter". He kills the pig and brings home the bacon while she cooks it up in a pan with all the laundry folded and put away and the kids tucked in by 8:30 pm every night. It is in fact a scientific brain design; males and females are better suited for certain tasks yet while we are certainly *not* limited to these primitive roles, it explains in a very basic way why men work so hard and why women obsess over caring for them. Women are attracted to and love to care for men that work hard, period. The harder they work, the more we scramble to care for them. A lazy man who cannot hunt is ugly.

A woman seeks a strong figure; after all, the extreme opposite is the figure who has achieved nothing; a homeless man for example. Women are not generally allured by a man who has not proven his worth through accomplishments just as some men find poor, needy women unattractive. It takes an awful lot of dedicated work to become rich. Speaking from experience and barring the authentic gold digger, his dedication and commitment are what engage women, not the actual money itself. These are the feelings and discussions I have shared between women in my circles since adulthood. We seem to all agree, his dedication and power over us and others are what make us most aroused. The money is evidence of his drive, is attractive and it makes a woman feel safer but it is his drive itself that makes her feel sexual. It is not enough to just be rich to make her fall for him. A guy that wins the lottery will attract gold diggers but he is not sexy unless he has accomplishments to accompany his money. There must be in him some element of intellect, philosophy or wisdom in order to make a woman truly and fully aroused. If he is poor however, it is enough to turn her off; that is, if he has no plans to acquire more money – *gross.* A poor man with drive is sexier than a rich man with a silver spoon up his ass. Notably in my personal experiences, I have never heard a woman speaking candidly and openly about "getting money" from a man although I have to assume the "gold digger" myth is real because I keep hearing about them. I don't know where they hang out nor do I know anything about their tactics. My player was one of a very short list of men I have asked for financial help from. Although rare, admittedly, each time it felt very gold-diggerish. Having your own money certainly feels a lot better.

His Intent

Why does a player play? Simply put; because he can. He suffers few repercussions because he does not extend time and energy being concerned with the exterior effects of his actions. He only concerns himself with tending to his own needs because this is what his relationships and society have tolerated. His is a learned behavior and one that works. He is allowed to enjoy a loving girlfriend experience with several women, yet he can attain this lop-sided dynamic without caring deeply for either of them. He doesn't have to because he knows women love for extended periods of time, even after they learn that the jig is up.

Further, playing women has become a conventional sport. Socially, it is accepted and sometimes even encouraged. It is considered much worse for a woman to take multiple suitors or engage in purely pleasure-seeking sexual experiences than it is for a man. The figurative Scarlett Letter still plainly brandishes its very disparaging mark on women in all types of media across all social margins. The world is not yet ready for the highly sexual biological female and thus throws her into a special category of humans; separate from the rest of society, she is shunned as the biblical leper, never to be allotted real love and intimacy. This degradation fuels the player culture by stamping the sexual female as a fair target. This is slut-shaming at its finest. She is no longer a "good girl" if she enjoys and seeks sex so you can play "that one" just for fun. This stigma becomes his loophole.

Today's hip hop culture, albeit very different from its origins, certainly paints a more detailed picture of this insecure sexual creature we call the female whore, never the woman who is secure in herself, not dramatic, not needy, a free spirit, poised with sexual prowess, flirtatious, at times strategically promiscuous and yet ever secure in her mental health. This character is by no means a myth and quite prevalent but she is also not popular; the only exception being if she is financially affluent. Somehow, in a very general social sense, if one is wealthy, one then transcends social labels. If she is wealthy and promiscuous, she becomes highly desirable and at the very least acceptable. If she is poor, she is a whore. Straight men have no such challenge in society so they can willfully seek out as many sex partners as they wish without risking being shamed because of it. I repeat; men play hearts because they can.

Ultimately, men need to feed their biological urges to be accepted sexually. Sexual gratification is how the male brain processes approval.

Without sexual gratification, his innate purposes in life can feel diluted. If a man cannot maintain healthy sexual relationships with the women or men he desires, he will have trouble processing his sense of masculinity; therefore, his sense of success. His intent then becomes one of self-gratification; finding glimpses of fulfillment in addictive behaviors like over-eating, drugs, alcohol, illicit sex or over-masturbating.

For the player, his sex relationships allow him the most control and he therefore pursues sexual pleasures as a part of his common lifestyle. He may find himself chasing more exciting or risky sex situations to enhance his sexual fulfillment; still void of any emotional attachments. He becomes an expert at managing and maintaining purely sexual relationships, especially with the type of women that become emotionally invested quickly. He will spend more energy upholding relations with an emotionally attached mark because her desperation, when he needs it, feeds his need to feel sexually desired. He is not prepared or willing to invest the work of a long-term relationship. If the relationship remains long-term, it is solely because the mark has decided to endure her situation and she holds the responsibility of staying on his radar. He does not pursue her. Since his position is socially accepted, the player does not consider his motives to be in any way morally unlawful. He plays on the love emotion because this gets his desired reaction and his participants have all been willing.

HER INTENT

Once a mark has fallen in love with a player, her intent is to force his emotional commitment. Whether she is aware of the game, she wants to feel loved and desired by him. She wants to capture his heart and mind by any means necessary. To this extent, she gives lavishly to her player; anything that she can offer. Women flaunt themselves to capture a man's heart. We show off our cooking, cleaning, intellect and artistic skills in order to coax our lovers into a higher appreciation of us. We use whatever tool we have including our beauty and bodies. The boundaries to which we flaunt ourselves are the tricky parts. How much of your body and mind should be sacrificed to lure a man's emotions? This spectrum of boundaries runs the gamut. Some women, at different stages in their lives, believe that giving sex may conjure his love and others believe withholding sex will achieve the same purpose. Is there a rule?

My mother told me that the key to a man's heart is through his stomach. "All you got to do is feed a man good and he'll marry you." Oddly, it worked for me. I cooked an immaculate Christmas dinner right before a man's eyes and hosted a great party where guests enjoyed turkey, fried chicken, collard greens, homemade biscuits, rice and gravy and a mean game of Yuletide Jeopardy. It was a blast and everything was delicious. My intent was to impress him enough to become betrothed. He asked me to marry him the next day. At the time, I thought that was a good thing. Today, however, I understand how perception works. Each woman has her own unique strategy of attraction and each man has his. Therefore, there can be no rules. The important thing to remember about the cards you've been handed is knowing when to fold 'em and when to hold 'em. Know when to walk away and know when to run. (Thank you, Kenny Rogers.) This means, learning how to place boundaries around yourself. Your boundaries will help you determine when to stop giving your precious energy to someone who can't receive it. Sometimes it isn't worth even putting on makeup for the world. Similarly, it isn't worth exerting any amount of energy on an impossible mission; namely, obliging someone to fall in love with you. When conventional love happens it is organic, mutual and easy to detect. It is something you cannot force.

In many ways a woman's femininity is steeped in her ability to care for others. Her sense of purpose often resides in her ability to effectively care for her children, parents and especially her love interests. If she does well caring for others, she feels confident in her every being. If she cannot maintain healthy relationships with the people in her life, she suffers mentally. A well-balanced woman understands and knows how to handle failure in relationships however, during her intervals of imbalanced emotional chemistry; she may have a very difficult time. In these cases, she uses her femininity to salvage any piece of the relationship that is important to her. When her bonds with her girlfriends are suffering, she might bring over ice cream and spend more time and energy into the relationship. In a love relationship, she may increase the quality or frequency of sex, text and call more, give gifts and so on; all in attempt to hold onto the relationship, even if it is toxic.

The mark's motives are emotional. Her ulterior motive is to control her player's thoughts and align them with hers. She wants him to think about her and often forces it; texting every night and morning for example. Doing this says, "I will force you to think about me every morning and every night." Boundaries are also an area where the mark can continually fail to exhibit her control. She essentially applies none when it comes to how deeply she allows herself to feel. It is this lack of boundaries that is at the root to a total *giving up* of emotional energy. This precise mechanism; that is, to be careful with our emotions, is what is missing when no boundaries are decided. A woman with no emotional boundaries cannot perceive the moment she passes from healthy to unhealthy thinking about her lover. She relents through all the red flags and gut feelings until in her fantasy she believes her player is feeling the same as her.

This is the great feminine danger. Women, being mainly wishful thinkers, imagine love is mutual every time they feel it, even if they suspect or even know the feeling is not mutual. This withholding of boundaries is the first stage of a long and painful illusion. Without setting your emotional boundaries at the beginning stages of any relationship, you are essentially jumping right down the figurative rabbit hole. You cannot conjure someone's love by giving yourself to them. It's not safe. Don't do it.

THE FAILURE

It has been established that the player in this game of seduction cannot lose. His game is not one that is won or lost. Even if he finds himself old, lonely and unable to locate a suitable mate, he need only to make the decision to continue the game or end it. There is no scorecard and records are not kept. Failure in this game is precluded by the player and any possible victories in this scenario are exclusive to him. The mark, on the other hand, is allowed only failure in the relationship. When nothing she does to promote growth of the relationship succeeds, she fails. When she becomes broken hearted, she fails. When she neglects responsibilities to tend to her emotional distress, she fails. Furthermore, if the pain she experiences is so severe that she closes her heart to love, she fails. If she takes her life, she fails. Ideally and typically, she will survive this with flying colors and subsequently learn from her experiences. It is a cosmic principle that although the gaining of success will be the result of a past failure, the failure itself nonetheless qualified as failure.

Once she fails in her emotional pursuits with her player, she now has a new challenge of applying what she knows to her physical pursuits, namely refusing to pick up her phone. The greatest struggle a woman battles as she let's go of her object of obsession is refraining from moving towards it. She may believe that if she exposes her pain to her player, it may persuade him to turn towards her or otherwise exact some kind of remorseful response. This could not be further from the truth. He is not concerned with her pain. He is avoiding it. The player, on hearing her proclaim pain will assume she is still available. To him, she is still interested if she is texting, calling, emailing or posting anecdotal blurbs on social media. It means she is still thinking about him and is a cue that he has the power to retake control of the relationship. Out of desperation she may try and push him away with words but it is important that she understand the clear conflict of interests in reaching towards someone whom your plan is to walk away from.

If she can come to regain her reality, that is, that her love relationship was a lie and that any love being felt was only felt by her, she can accept the fantasy of hope and the reality of a new plan. In other words, she has to let go of the fantasy of her player's love so that she can move in a safe direction. If she holds onto this false hope, she cannot fully conceive nor justify severing her connection with him. Her need to contact her player stems simply from hope. She hopes he is different despite his consistent inappropriate actions, words and gestures. Losing hope is difficult in any situation whether it be for a child, a parent or loved one. In this case, she loves him which is why ceasing all contact is the mark's ultimate fear. It is the painful marker of her secession from love to the acceptance of failure.

It took me countless tries over several years to finally cease contacting my player. There had been a series of discoveries about him and myself each time I said goodbye. The first was riddled with the unsettling notion that he was not who he had appeared to be. It was my greatest heartbreak. It was on February 4th; a Tuesday night. My children were with their father as was the case every Tuesday, so I could cry as loud as I wanted. I had seen him a few days prior for about an hour or so. He had been completely inebriated and did not remember telling me that he was a whore and he did not care about my pain despite the tears that streamed down my face uncontrollably. I was too proud to bawl in front of him and I tried to keep a straight face but I could not stop the tears. Everything hurt. Later, I learned that he had been drunk enough to have no recollection of the entire conversation. He did not remember that I had cried and I was glad. The next day, I made a choice. We had not yet engaged in sexual intercourse and I had been contemplating whether I would. Once I realized he was not the "pair-bonding" type, it was clear. I could either walk away with the uncertainty of what could have been or I could release all of my expectations and move towards him, settling my curiosities. I chose to move towards him. Although we had not yet had intercourse, we had shared some physical intimacy which proved to me he was a skilled and confident lover. I invited him over. I was already in love so my plan was to experience him for as long as I could stand it. I was too controlled by both physical lust and emotional love to make a fair decision and I failed at this first attempt to say goodbye.

The second attempt was about a month later. It was very clear from the restart that nothing had changed. He was just as rude and uncaring as he had been. I realized very quickly that I was too emotionally attached to have a no-strings sexual relationship with him. When I was in his presence, I felt amazing. Despite his behaviors, I felt special around him. My brain would become flooded with dopamine from looking at him, taking in his scent, touching him and hearing his voice among other things. He gave me great pleasure but it hurt something terrible when he was away because all I could think about was that he did not care that I missed him. So, I said goodbye again. During that time, I knew full well who and what I was dealing with. I also knew that if I let him back in, I would get hurt all over again. Another failure was looming in fast.

I went back in; all in for five months. I saw him every chance I got and flooded my brain with fantasies of him when we weren't together. Most were sexual but occasionally I would visualize pillow talk and engage in imaginary conversations. It was insanity and it fueled my emotional demise because it allowed me to tolerate his uncaring behaviors and words. It was a stealthy balance of pleasure and stress that made seeing him bearable. At each emotional failure when I became hurt, I would use my fantasies like a drug. I knew he didn't love me. I was addicted to the feeling it gave me to think about being with him. The sweetness of my thought life seemed to overshadow the sourness of the real world. It was yet another miserable and necessary failure.

A mark in love with a player has already failed. Once she is aware, she must decide whether she will stay or go. She must determine when her series of failures should end over him. If she decides to leave, she must constantly remind herself that the relationship is over and more importantly that her suffering is only in her head and nowhere else. It will not spill over into anyone else's life, especially not his. It is not important that he be made aware of how much pain she is in. Ceasing contact with her player is her best course of action and from my experience, the most difficult one to take.

THE VICTORY

The victory in this game is only awarded to the player. The mark is always handed failure because the rules are stacked against her. The victory is won when the player receives his mark's sexual and/or emotional cooperation while giving her his bare minimum. If he can achieve immunity for his behaviors while continuing to maintain her attention, he wins. If she leaves before getting emotionally hooked, he simply moves on to try again. There is no loss. His endeavor is insatiable because what he is after is continual reassurance that he is desirable. There is no end game.

CHAPTER 3 | THE BIOLOGY OF THE GAME

Recognizing the pliability of the neurological-self is paramount to overcoming the dogmatism of the psychological-self.

After studying neurology on my own I decided to take a psychology course online from The University of Toronto and scored a 94% overall. After that I took a genetics course online from The University of Michigan and scored a 96%. I felt like a smart ass again. I also wanted to gain a full understanding of how the brain was involved in the mind and physical body. What I learned was so amazingly awesome I swear at one point I had to jump up and down because I thought I was going to explode. Who has Autism now? Additionally, I generally toiled with how much *actual science* I would impart in this book. There is far too much valuable information to fit all in one book so picking apart the pertinent bits was like trying to pick the best red M&M out of a thousand red M&Ms when all of them are delicious. Originally, I wrote this chapter as a very scientific piece. It was sterile, boring as hell and oddly stood out from the other chapters. I had written about thirty pages on the structure of the brain, neurohormones and some other very intricate details on brain function. All of it seemed jumbled, out of context and generally not funny or even interesting. Further, it had nothing to do with players. What I was trying to do was give the reader a crash course on basic neuroscience. The idea being, if you fully understood how your brain is put together and how it works, common sense would suddenly shed some miraculous light into your situation. "Ah ha!" you would say. "It was the dopamine and oxytocin!" you might proclaim. "It all makes sense to me now!" Certainly, just knowing these very interesting details about how our brains perceive should automatically set everyone straight, right? Not quite. The trouble is, thirty pages into this chapter, I hadn't mentioned "player" once. It was neither effective writing nor good teaching. I felt it was extremely important to pick apart the brain in a very specific way so the reader would fully understand the psychological implications, but I had failed to make the information relatable and easy to read. My friend and neuroscientist, Dr. Brian King carefully advised however, that I might consider reducing some of the information I crammed into it because it was confusing as hell. Frustrated, I scrapped the whole damned chapter and started rewriting this paragraph. Thank you, Dr. Brian King. You were right.

While it is important that you understand some basics of how your brain works in order to put all your emotions and experiences into a healthy perspective, it really makes no sense to bore you with a full-on neurology lesson. Admittedly, it was painful to forego explanations of brain-based electromagnetism, neurons and high cognitive functions, emotive responses, the neuroendocrine system among other truly fascinating processes in the brain. That said, however happy I am about being a nerd, I'll try my best to focus on the most relevant and fascinating aspects of how the human brain works inside this player-mark relationship. I also want the discovery of brain science to be a relatable journey; one you can understand and apply. Therefore, appropriately I'll start with my personal discovery of neuroscience.

My twenties were care-free in the 90's and I felt like a hippie that was twenty years too late. I drank too much and moved around the city a lot. Although raised in a Christian home in the south, I was open to reading theology and history; a big no-no where I'm from. (It's deep.) By age twenty-two I was consuming heaps of fluffy self-help books, most of which I was completely satisfied with. I fell into every paragraph with whole-heartedness and upon flipping the last pages I always felt like I was getting somewhere. Each book seemed to give me a new perspective on my chaotic past. That was all well but at age thirty-seven, having newly separated from my husband and my second child, then age two and newly carrying a label of Autism; I began to read books about the brain. I was a complete, depressive wreck with two children to care for all by myself. It felt hopeless and suicide wasn't an option. Brain control was my only hope at that stage when it came to coping with my past, divorce, financial straits and especially when I was interacting with my Autistic daughter. Neurology research proved the most effective move. It felt like killing a whole lot of birds with one stone.

At the time, I desperately needed to understand what my daughter might be experiencing so I read. There were many layers to gaining an understanding of her Autism but I only learned about how the brain worked cognitively; in other words, how we learn and remember new skills, how speech works and some motor functions. As a mother, it was paramount to finding a tool by which I would be able to communicate with and effectively mother my daughter. She could not talk at age three; a year after the marriage ended and I knew I wouldn't be able to speak her language until I understood how her brain was interpreting the world. From what I researched and from some of the techniques I picked up from her therapists, I learned how to teach her to communicate. My experience was a best-case scenario.

Until she was three, she was overwhelmed by some of what she saw, heard, touched and smelled and would occasionally react by covering her eyes and ears, then hit the ground making growling noises. I couldn't understand it even after I learned what Autism was. None of the clues seemed to paint a full picture of what we were up against and further, there was no consistent or real-life definition of Autism. It is a spectrum disorder meaning, symptoms vary, conditions vary; everything varies. Everything was confusing. Second and third opinions seemed meaningless as we ended up feeling empty-handed after each doctor's visit. Main stream medicine is a hell of an industry. When I went out on my own and came to know the basic functions of the brain, much of what I had learned about Autism began to make sense. I now had something tangible that I could apply. I no longer felt helpless.

Early on in my cognitive brain journey, I figured out creative ways to teach my daughter how to break a one syllable word apart so she could speak it. The first word I taught her to say was book. If I said, "Peyton, say book,' she would say "cup" consistently. From what I had learned about the brain, I was able to observe that she seemed to have trouble putting together smaller audible parts to make a whole audible part. One day, I asked her to repeat the B sound, then the OO sound and finally the K. Over and over we practiced this. It was new and seemed to frustrate my older daughter who was six at the time. Perhaps it was too repetitive and forced. At any rate, after about fifteen or twenty minutes, Peyton combined all three sounds and said the full word. "B-OO-K," she said, or more like "Booooook". It worked. Suddenly, she understood all of what I was trying to do and it became easier to teach her to say words this way. Once she learned how to communicate, she became a different child. All it took was a little neuroscience and mothering. I was onto something. I bought a few more books about the brain and started seeking out brain articles online. It became a hobby and somewhere into the middle of my third or fourth neuroscience read I went to my bookshelf, threw out all the stupid, ridiculous books that I had once loved in my early twenties and then went to make a turkey sandwich. It was sweet relief.

Neuroscience is amazing and for me, clearly was the answer to all the piercing questions I had, not only about how to teach and raise both my daughters but how to come to terms with everything I struggled with in the past, present and presumably my future. Brain science was the mother of all answers barring religious platforms since we have to ultimately account for who or what could have designed such an amazing tool as the human brain; or any brain for that matter. With a handful of books under my belt, I was able to analyze the pieces to why I had failed in many of my relationships and goals. I could finally put in some logical perspective all the bad thinking, eating and drinking I had done. Ultimately, it had been about fear. There was a full story around all of it that was far deeper and more reaching than any single bad decision I had made. I realized that there was an actual biological and chemical story happening inside our heads and spinal cords that is linked to our histories. There is no separating your physical history from your emotional history. Biology is like the musician Chris Brown. It's everywhere and you can't get away from it. Try to ignore it for twenty-four hours and you'll fail miserably.

After reading *The Male Brain* by Dr. Lauann Brizendine, I realized that I had men pegged completely wrong and so do most women; all due to a complete neglecting of biology. In turn, it became perfectly clear that men must be outright and utterly bewildered by women. Knowing what I now knew suddenly made me sad. I felt like the whole world had been bamboozled into thinking men and women and people in general were all supposed to be similar. *Boooooo!*

There were multitudes of "Ah-ha!" moments; like being on an educational joy ride. It all suddenly made sense because everything seemed to boil down to brain chemicals. Before my "brain journey" I had come to a dysfunctional understanding about the world. I believed that people just did evils things and that I would just have to figure out how to endure it at some abhorrent cost. I'm stuck here, I thought. (Secretly, I have been waiting for my alien family to come rescue me.) Suddenly, when I learned the mechanics of why people do and think, it almost took the sting completely out of everybody's bullshit. (Although if my alien family were to show up; I'm leaving.) I even learned about the law of attraction and have come to understand the part I played in the evil I allowed in my life. Since my searches for answers lead me straight to neuroscience, the first order of business is to help you understand the differences between the male and female brain and the respective strategies they use to process attraction, lust, sex, love and a few other social behaviors.

THE HUMAN BRAIN

The brain drives everything we do and defines our perception of everything we experience and feel. Perception is the key word that I want you to consider throughout all of what you learn herein. Your brain is supreme and should be your most cosseted tool because when it breaks, so will the rest of you. Your perception of the world and yourself is all you have. If you plan on ending a toxic relationship, you had better understand what you're up against; internally that is. In other words, ask yourself, "What is my brain going to do once I make this extremely difficult decision?" "How will seeing him affect me?" or "How will not seeing him affect me?" All of these are important questions; in fact, every good scientist knows that good science generates good questions. Asking yourself questions about your own brain will be your best defense against any debacle because your brain is your figurative *everything*. It is what allows you to perceive everything around you. It is the reason you can feel joy, love or more appropriately, brokenhearted.

In simple terms, the brain's operations work using a combination of chemicals and processes. Similar to the way a computer works, your brain uses hard-wired circuitry and electromagnetic signals carrying information from one part to another. Computers use strategy and math to generate information and do cool stuff, like produce data and videos. The difference is that circuitry networks in the brain use the synergy of strategy and math to do cool stuff, like create feeling and action. The most helpful part is while chemicals make you feel and do stuff, they can also change based on your own thoughts and behavior. It is the yin and yang of bio-emotion. One affects the other and vice versa. This phenomenon of a constant changing, building, destroying and rearranging of brain matter based on what we do and think is a true testament of how temporal our problems are. We have a capacity to withstand high levels of physical and emotional stress and our brain seems to continually evolve physically to assist and survive. This is real hope in knowing that new experiences will shape and reshape your brain to position you for all your goals, including ending a noxious relationship.

A Brief History

The field of neuroscience has expanded by volumes in the last two decades. Twenty-five years ago, technology had given scientists a glimpse into the brain with the use of magnetic resonance imaging more widely known as MRI. Unlike x-rays, MRI is suited for imaging non-bony or soft tissue regions in the body and can differentiate between white matter and grey matter in the brain. Until recently, this technology was fledging and expensive which thwarted brain research as a whole. Incidentally, the model of the majority of brain research centered on the male brain and did little dealings with the female brain at all. It was considered more economical to study the male brain in a male centered culture since it had been presumed that female brains were too complicated. (Now *that* is pretty player.) In the world of neuroscience, the male brain held the authority however as research expanded, we have learned of blatantly stark differences between male and female brains. In a 1996 study conducted about empathy, scientists Gallese and Rizzolatti discovered that the female brain processes empathy not only in a different hemisphere of the brain than the male's, but it also uses a different strategy altogether. Additionally, you can hold up a male brain against its female counterpart and tell which one is a boy, just like you would a puppy. It is a miracle that any relationship could work considering the differences of how males and females experience love and life. In fact, conventional marriage almost feels like a set-up once you realize how different the sexes are.

Since its development in the late 70's, the MRI has led to the development of more economical and therefore readily available technologies. Today, a new iteration of MRI, the functional MRI (or fMRI) has allowed neurology to move into a new era of research. It can be used to determine which brain regions and neurohormones are responsible for handling critical functions. Doctors can also monitor the effects of stroke or disease and the fMRI is essential for treatment of the brain. This technology uses magnetic resonance to capture blood flow and the consumption of oxygen which defines "activity" or metabolic changes within the brain. The more blood flow in an area of the brain means more brain activity is occurring. This has enabled scientists to see functionally what is happening in the brain while it is problem solving, retrieving a memory, telling a lie, falling in love, playing with a child, reading facial expressions and experiencing a range of emotions. Because of this, neuroscience has been able to determine neurological profiles for a wide range of specific physical action and emotive response. For example, when a person is falling in love, his or her brain activity changes and therefore looks different than a brain that is not in love. When a person is walking, certain areas of the brain "light up" and specific chemicals are released. The stressful brain appears and functions very differently to one that is at peace. Inference about a person's psychological tendencies can be made by observing how their brain behaves on the fMRI. It has uncovered a clear connection between a person's mental health and the strategies their brain uses to process stress. The fMRI has subsequently brought about a long and overdue amalgamation of biochemistry, neuroscience and psychology. It's about time.

HOW IT WORKS

Neurohormones are chemicals produced by certain organs like the brain, testicles, ovaries and adrenal glands, among others, and travel through the brain via tiny *neural pathways*. Their purpose is to either excite or inhibit other chemicals which will in turn create an action and/or physical or emotional feeling in the body. The neurohormone either prevents or accelerates *neurotransmitters* and through a set of electromagnetic chain reactions can stimulate a beating heart, a reaching arm or that feeling in your gut that the person you're in love with doesn't love you back. Neurohormones can also serve the role of neurotransmitter which transmits signals across the neurons and over the bridges in the brain called *synapse.* Transmitters give the final instruction on what action the mind and body should take.

To illustrate the hormonal relationships in the brain, imagine you are looking at map of the whole world chopped full of highways, intersections and bridges. A city on this map could be a village of like-minded people, representing a neuron. Cars traveling along these highways carry precious cargo representing the messages that are carried to and from the body and brain. The vehicles characterize neurohormones constantly moving across the map. Interestingly, some vehicles have special privileges. Only vehicles whose plates are licensed as "neurotransmitters" can continue on across the bridges and even go off road. These messenger cars are special and must collect and deliver tons of mail and cover a wide range of turf while the unmarked cars (regular old neurohormones) go about doing their jobs traveling up and down a few highways, dropping off mail just a few miles from home.

Just as our national infrastructure works, if two highways are used often enough, a bridge is built between the two for convenience. When you use the same brain circuits repeatedly, a synapse is literally created in the brain between two active neural pathways. Synapses are the areas between neural pathways just where they connect. Although it can look like these highways in the brain are touching, the synapse is actually an empty space where signals bounce back and forth, transferring information kind of like what happens between your remote control and your television. This new bridge makes the highways, intersections and messenger cars all work together more effectively to deliver messages to the body.

In the brain, these networks also work together to specifically accommodate a particular task if it has been repeated enough times. This is how we become experts. The brain actually changes shape to facilitate you becoming an expert at anything you do over and over again. Eventually, if a person becomes an expert at a task, his or her brain will have formed thousands of tiny bridges and intersections, connecting a densely rooted "mapping" of brain functionality associated with that specific task. Experts therefore use true, tried and tested "profiles" in the brain each time they are engaged in their area of expertise. That includes all the emotional conditioning associated with being either the player or the mark.

Neurohormones are released into the bloodstream to spawn systematic effects on your mind and body. The main players inside the male brain start with testosterone, vasopressin, oxytocin, prolactin, cortisol, dopamine and estrogen. The female brain is driven by a slightly different combination; namely estrogen, progesterone, testosterone, oxytocin, cortisol, vasopressin and DHEA. Although males and females share many of the same primary hormones, there are significant differences in their dosage and synergetic affects. The results of these differences are what define us as male, female or transgender. These recipes can also distinguish our personalities as aggressive, passive or indifferent. Hormones in a way decide how we think. If your hormones are off balance, so are you. Chemicals therefore play a specific role in your detection, perception and processing of pain; both physical and emotional.

Think of it as if we were made from a recipe book by someone who never measures when they cook, like me. This is why I don't do well at baking but every time I cook fried chicken it is delicious. May I remind you that I am southern? May I also add that my mother is a large black woman whose father was a sharecropper? They became accustomed to cooking without certain utensils (like measuring cups and clocks) and as a child, my grandmother taught me to listen for when fried chicken was done all the way through. "He'll quiet down like he's trying to hide. That's when you know he's ready," she told me. Although my fried chicken always tastes good, it doesn't always taste the same because I don't measure or look at clocks when I cook. Some batches have a little more salt than others; sometimes more or less flour or none at all. I would only use egg in the batter when I felt fancy. Each batch, although certainly fried chicken, had a different set of ingredients that created a different effect on how it tasted and felt in your mouth. Always delicious, but never the same; kind of like the human race. Men and women are generally the same but our hormonal recipes are different and we clearly have been created by a cook that doesn't measure because none of us match exactly. In the brain, each hormone has its own set of unique purposes and each creates very different and specialized systematic effects. When you understand what some are designed to do; especially when combined with each other, it is easy to understand how the totality of the network of male versus female neurohormones shapes how differently we think and feel. This will help you navigate through emergency and emotional pain.

With all the information that is stored in your brain, if someone yells, "Fire!" your brain releases a chemical called cortisol, a stress hormone which within milliseconds, floods the bloodstream. Cortisol causes your body to pull all pertinent resources together; namely strengthening muscle groups and brain regions that control mental focus plus whatever else it takes to help you detect the fire and move your ass out of the way as stupendously as possible. Therefore, it has to also simultaneously cause other unnecessary body functions to cease for example; digestion or your blink reflex. Instead of spending energy breaking down your lunch, you'll use that energy moving your ass out of the way as stupendously as possible. All psychological and physiological action stems from the combination of brain chemicals and how they are processed; talking, walking, feeling emotion, habitual behaviors, involuntary actions and so on. A person's psychological-self is a direct symptom of their neurological-self; therefore, your brain holds center authority on every single thing you do and feel.

How We Learn

After reading this section, my hope is that you will understand how the mark and the player learned so well to play their respective games. I'll explain on a very basic level how the brain facilitates learning which applies to mastering the alphabet as a toddler all the way through to adulthood when learning to love yourself and others.

A baby is shown a flashcard of a red bird. He hears his mother say, "Red bird." In his brain, the highway controlling his hearing registers the sound. Simultaneously, the highway controlling vision registers the image of the red bird on the flashcard. If his mother repeats this action enough times, these two highways will form a bridge; the synapse connecting them. Every time he sees that flashcard, the neurological mapping he created with his mother will light up. If this happens enough times, he'll quickly become a pro at recognizing the flashcard and maybe even spotting red birds in his neighborhood. When the baby encounters other red objects and hears the word "red", he will develop a differential between objects and their description as other more specific mapping occurs and new synapse are formed, thus separating "red" from "bird". He is learning through the creation of other neural connections that birds, tables and cars can all be red. He will learn that birds also exist in colors other than red. When stimulated with familiarity, his neural connections will remind him of what he has learned and he becomes a master at distinguishing the color red and the category of bird from other colors and creatures. This basic brain operation directly explains why practice makes perfect. This also applies all the way into maturity when developing healthy sexual relationships.

Memory enables us to learn through recalling past experiences using the brain's natural reward system of pleasure and pain. Further, although reluctant to change behavioral infrastructure, the brain is and will always be changing shape until death. The purpose of this continual change is to better adapt us to our current environments. Your brain is using memory in a constant fight to preserve the *same-same*; reinforcing itself to help you maintain life with little disruption. It wants to get you used to whatever is in front of you. In fact, when your routines drastically change, the brain is affected causing the body to likewise be affected until the new changes are no longer new. That is, with time and repetition, we can become accustomed to almost anything; good or bad. Learning about how the individual parts of our brain change our thinking is important to overcoming the overwhelming affects that disruption places on our emotional well-being, especially when it comes to heartbreak.

I want to remind you to place all this scientific goodness into perspective. We're feeding our brains constantly; whether good or bad, something is going in and we are learning. Classic Conditioning is a psychology term used to explain how creatures learn through repetition. A mouse can be taught to push a red button to request food. If placed in a box with a red and a green button, it doesn't take a hungry mouse long to get creative and starting trying everything he's got. Eventually, he'll stumble across the red button and learn that if pushed, a food pellet will drop into his box. Simultaneously, he ignores the green button which produces no food. He learns through his repetitive experiences so that every time he is exposed to any red buttons, he automatically tries to push for food. Humans are the same way. If your player keeps pushing for food and getting fed, what would stop him from continuing to push? Like the mouse, he would need to push the button a gang of times until he's convinced it no longer works. It can take some time but eventually he will stop trying. Woman up and turn your buttons off ladies.

THE FIVE PARTS OF THE BRAIN

Although I fought tooth and nail to spare you this very technical section, ultimately, I realized that I didn't really want to spare you so I'm including it. Plus, I'm divorced, 43 years old with two kids and I can do whatever I want. To reduce the size of this section, I removed the spacing between each paragraph and used a smaller font. Then, I clicked undo, used the correct formatting, threw my hands in the air and said, "To hell with it." At any rate, I predict that if you skip this section, it may haunt you in your dreams so take no chances and at least skim through it. I couldn't bear to leave any of it out because all these sultry parts are so interesting and all gooey and delicious in fact the bits I did remove are sitting right down in the damned glossary. This is particularly why it is considered that scientists and science scholars are not good writers. It is because eventually they have to bore you with the details and it is very difficult to make intricate science interesting. So, I am simply disclosing the reason why I'm about to bore you to death for the next three pages. Nevertheless, after reading them you may forget the five parts of the brain and how they function. You should, however gain a better understanding of how your experiences, memory and learning capabilities affect your emotions before, during and after any relationship.

The human brain is separated into five major sections and is divided into four "lobes", called the frontal lobe, parietal lobe, temporal lobe and occipital lobe. These four lobes make up the larger majority of the brain called the cerebrum. The fifth section, the limbic system, is unique and stands apart by its structure and functionality. To remember this, I think of a human hand with five digits altogether, four of which are similar and the fifth; the thumb, is strange and has a unique purpose.

THE LIMBIC SYSTEM

Our *limbic system* is where our emotions start. The underbelly of the cerebrum; spanning from the bottom of the frontal lobe to the inner sections of the temporal lobes and then to the back of the brain that attaches to the spinal cord; this area controls the origination of emotive response. It combines high mental function like learning and forming memory with primitive emotion like love and fear into one cohesive system. This is the part of the brain that lights up when we are falling in or out of love, stressed or feeling pleasure and is therefore sometimes referred to as our emotional nervous system. It is an oddball area that we'll discuss often.

FRONTAL LOBE

The *frontal lobe* sits right behind the forehead at the front of the brain and helps regulate behavior, learning, and voluntary movement. It supervises our capacities in speaking, thinking, making decisions and planning and is the real source of an individual's personality. It is closely linked to memory and sensory centers in the brains and its primary job is to allow us to think things through and determine how to use the information we've stored in other parts of the brain. The frontal lobe contains most of the dopamine-sensitive neurons in the brain. Dopamine is what causes us to feel all types of pleasure and is also responsible for our determination of what is considered "normal".

PARIETAL LOBE

As all the four components of the cerebrum, the *parietal lobe* is structured with left and right hemispheres. Starting from the top of your head, it extends down, deep behind the eyes. It situates behind the frontal lobe and above the occipital lobe just under the parietal bone of the skull. Its main function includes the handling of sensory information like hearing, touch, taste, temperature and navigation as well as some processing of language.

TEMPORAL LOBE

The *temporal lobes* are located just on the other side of each ear and appropriately handle auditory processing. This region also helps us establish visual memories and is therefore almost solely responsible for language recognition and comprehension and plays a key role in coordinating with the hippocampus (in the very emotional *limbic system*) to develop explicit long-term memory moderated by the amygdala (also in the limbic system). The hippocampus and amygdala are closely related; managing memory and emotion so the temporal region helps us interpret the meaning and memory information from what we hear and see. It helps us recognize objects and sounds and then form an emotional value to them, or not. If we do form emotional values to what we see and hear, we have a greater chance of remembering what was observed in fact studies have found that when scientists administer cortisol (stress hormone) to individuals directly after having learned something, they are more likely to recall that information later on. When emotional value is not attached to our experiences, the information is essentially pushed out of the brain to make room for more significant memories.

OCCIPITAL LOBE

The *occipital lobe* is the member of the cerebrum that sits at the very back of the brain. It is primarily associated with vision. Sensory input from the eyes travels through the entire brain, passing through a nucleus that also processes other sensory messages like taste, temperature, sound and touch. The visual signals then move to and through the occipital lobes which translates the raw visual input into a message that allows us to identify what we are looking at. When you are observing an object, there are two basic processes that happen; first you process its characteristics like shape, color and size. Second, you identify the object by name. People with deficiencies in this area of the brain can pick out the characteristics of an object while looking at it; for example, identifying something is blue and round, but once you hand them the object, allowing them to process a combined sensory through vision and touch, *only then* can they identify it as, "A ball!" This highly interesting condition is called Visual Agnosia and once literally caused a man to mistake his wife for a hat. He reached out and upon touching her head, his brain reminded him that she was not his hat.

This, the last paragraph in a section that has nothing directly to do with players is over. Now you have a basic understanding of how the brain's networks work together to produce life as you know it. Congratulations. The take away here is to understand the gravity in altering the chemistry or structure of the brain especially when processing emotion. In this game of life, humans as a species are basically the same. We require food, water, shelter and love; however, differences in brain function between the sexes should also be considered as we navigate the dynamics of men that play hearts to break them.

THE MALE BRAIN

Male and female brains fundamentally differ down to the very cells that make them up. The cells in a male's brain and body contain the Y chromosome but the female's does not. This small difference is the rudder that drives male and female neurological and physiological development in two almost totally different directions. Within seven to eight weeks of gestation, this Y chromosome causes the male fetus to form testicles which flood the brain with enough testosterone to permanently alter its developmental framework and structure.

As humans, our species share operating systems so some male to female body functions are identical. We all have a heart and it beats; we all use one stomach to digest food; we develop opposable thumbs and we can also perform mental reasoning. These tell-tale activities define us as human but obvious physical differences; namely, vaginas and penises, should also illustrate the stark neurological and psychological differences between men and women. Just as our bodies are equipped differently, so are our brains therefore naturally we develop two very different lenses through which we continually experience life. Wisely, we must remind ourselves of this. Men and women both feel "love" but we feel it differently. Men fall in love using a totally different neural planning than women. We both understand empathy but again, process it with an opposite hemisphere of the brain and with a different strategy. Socially, if you are aware of these differences, it is very easy to understand why women think men are stupid and men think women are crazy. As I'll explain throughout this chapter, neither group is correct. We are merely different. The reason for the disparities between how men and women use their brains lies in the unique neurohormones each sex manufactures to manage how we feel, act and develop as adults.

Due to male hormonal urges, many males organically become the player without intending or even knowing it. The player, therefore, is not as uncommon as most might assume. Typically, a man can very easily seek to continue a sexual relationship with a woman who is deeply in love with him, even if he is not in love with her. He only needs to enjoy her company. He does not need to care about her deeply. His neurochemistry facilitates this arrangement quite conveniently in fact it takes an awful lot of work and time for the male brain to develop feelings of love as compared to women. If he is being satisfied sexually, it is easy for him to give less attention to ancillary challenges like her hurt feelings, for example. Additionally, if he is able to maintain her sexual connectedness in a way that avoids his discomfort, he will continue to see her even if it causes her deep emotional pain. He doesn't have to be a player to pull this off. For many men, if there is guilt about his lover's emotional pain, it may not be enough for him to stop the sexual relationship. He may begin calling or texting less often but will at the least attempt to have sex. Males weigh their sexual activities against a woman's hurt feelings and sometimes, sex wins. The player's sexual convenience means very much to him. Besides, her pain is out of sight and therefore out of mind. If she does not challenge his emotions, never asks too many questions and rarely argues, he will have no reason to do anything differently. This is in no way *player*. This is simply *male* and she has created a much-desired arrangement for any regular guy, much more for the player. A man will not usually end any behavior until the behavior becomes a strain on him.

The avoidance of emotions is a male human characteristic because the tending to emotions is both forbidden in his culture and positively stressful to his brain circuitry. His plane of emotion does not reflect his level of intelligence; nor does it reflect his ability to feel. He simply feels like men feel as women feel like women feel; in two totally different ways. If she allows his neglectful behaviors, he'll get very comfortable, no matter how he feels about her. This is human nature and player or not, men have a propensity for doing things efficiently and effectively with no fat on the bones. Whatever is allowed will continue.

Maintaining strictly sexual relationships with women who are in love with them seems an ambitious goal that certainly won't work every time. Not all women will create the environment that facilitates such emotional debauchery. The cold truth is that I, along with a lot of other damaged individuals, accidently threw a very expensive player-friendly party and invited the wrong motherfucker. A man can easily become a player for the first time within this inductive environment. His male biology is designed to seek masculinity through sex. Create the right environment for him and he will find you.

MEN ARE DIFFERENT, NOT STUPID

Let's face it. Women call men stupid behind their backs and men think women are crazy right out in the open. Is there a settlement to this most controversial argument? Could both sides be right? Maybe we've got it backwards. Are women stupid and men the crazy ones? Not exactly, in fact neither is correct and I intend to illustrate why. Let's start with why men aren't stupid.

After birth, boys and girls do not differ much in terms of their outward development. A boy's face and body will not develop masculinity until about age six. From the ages of nine and fifteen, boys experience puberty and receive surges of the very male hormones; testosterone and vasopressin. While each have their specific purposes, the combination of these two neurohormones creates an explosion of sexually charged physical and mental development. The testosterone will promote the growth of his testicles, body hair and muscles, widen and lengthen his penis, lower his voice and activate regions of the brain that control sexual pursuit and aggression. It will send signals to his brain when he sees a woman's breasts and male or female body parts that activate the hypothalamus and cause his frontal lobe – the area of the brain that controls the "forefront" of his thoughts – to be flooded with these images. Vasopressin is, in fact, the male "love" hormone and therefore further contributes to his new obsession with sex. Boys often account to feeling like a pervert during this phase of his life. He may be or feel a little pervy but he is also *perv-ectly* normal. (No one laughed. Not even me.) When his hypothalamus is under the onslaught of vasopressin and testosterone together, his brain circuits become so focused on sexual pursuit and pleasure while other parts of his brain simply deactivate. Reckless behavior often follows. If mothers of teenage boys understood neurologically what is happening to their sons, surely it would lessen the nuisance of parenting an adolescent male. Fathers on the other hand, have been through it already. The trick is learning how to control the pervy before you grow all the way up. Teenage perv is to *normal*; as adult perv is to *ew*. Good luck fellas.

If we refer again to the brain map illustration, we become aware that there is more than one route to any destination. If the freeway is closed, we take the streets or a flight or even a boat so long as we get there. This is the same basic application with the way male and female brains work. We can experience the same range of relative emotions; however, by nature we often use a different method and route to get there and therefore it feels very different.

Often new mothers become frustrated at their husbands for not jumping into action when their baby needs help. Whether she verbalizes her frustration, she may think, "How could he have strapped our only child in the car seat without noticing she was uncomfortable? If *he* were sitting like this wouldn't *he* want to be helped? For God's sake it's cold. What an idiot," as she carefully props baby upright, stuffs a pillow under her chin for extra support and fixes her shirt and jacket. This mother interprets her husband as being neglectful based on her own inclinational standards. She judges him against what she would have done naturally. Her aggression cues trigger and if she challenges him, dad will certainly have a hard time finding a leg to stand on. After all, it hadn't occurred to him that baby looked uncomfortable until she pointed it out. In all his frustration and also upon watching her fix the baby, he can now mathematically deduce that clearly the baby's shirt was exposing her belly to the cold air and her head was hanging at a strange angle as she slept. Additionally, he is fully aware of his wife's expectation that he should have noticed. And of course, when challenged, masculinity requires that he decide whether any battle is won or lost. If his wife has expected him to perform something impossible, like reading a sleeping baby's mind for example, he may see no solution. He can only reassess his problem to not be a lack of clairvoyance but, if for a fleeting moment, that his wife is in fact a witch in all forms of the word.

If mom speaks up and fusses at him about the baby's discomfort, which by the way he cannot actually detect; his brain reacts, forcing him into defense mode thinking; "Why doesn't she just fix the baby and shut up! Besides, the baby is asleep and is therefore likely comfortable as hell, you crazy biiiiiiiiiitch!" Whatever comes out of his mouth causes an argument and likely wakes the baby. Suddenly he's a bumbling fool in her eyes. This very battle-of-the-sexes type of scenario plays out time and time again and illustrates many of the emotional and cognitive differences between males and females; namely the visual processing of facial expressions and fine details, empathy, anger and of course our contrasting aptitude for turning emotions into words. If he knew how her brain worked, he might take extra care to fluff the baby a little after he straps her into the car seat next time. If she knew how his brain worked, she would have just fixed the baby and taken extra care to shut it. Neither is wrong. Neither is right. The point is, as a team they got the baby home safely. Nature wins.

The issue, if fully exposed, is in the brain and has nothing to do with intelligence or witchcraft. It all boils down to the primal concept of men being suited for hunting and women for gathering. While there are exceptions to any rule, the female is specifically wired for empathy, to notice fine details and become stressed or moved emotionally when something is wrong with another person or animal. To a man, this ability to feel what others feel seems like a mythical super power he cannot relate to, does not consider nor does he expect it to become a part of his life on any day. It looks crazy, sounds crazy and yet, he relies on it when he needs a woman's intuition and insight. He especially relied on it as a child while his mother was raising him. These are of the great mysteries of life. Just as there comes a point in every man's life where he feels somewhat slighted because a woman has seemingly read his mind; every woman has also been offended because a man has failed to return this supernatural favor. Clearly there is a vital disconnect between how the sexes relate. Could it be scientific? Of course it is. When you pick it apart, it is rather condescending that society has assumed stupidity onto men and insanity onto women when measuring their differences. Stupid is a stretch. So is crazy. Use your brain. Different will do just fine, thank you.

The amalgamation of physiological and neurological differences between males and females creates a most contrasting life experience for each which often leads to general misinterpretations between the two. What typically occurs to each sex within any given set of circumstances will likely be different. Neither is wrong. Each sex is experiencing a different sensory and perception experience; just as individuals are unique in their perspectives and opinions. While we are human, there are more similarities between male and female neurological structure and function than differences however, the synergy and significance of the differences creates an almost opposite interpretation of life and purpose.

SEX & EMOTION

To a woman, the male brain seems quite peculiar when it comes to sex. There is a special part of the brain called the hypothalamus which is the real root behind what initially drives a man to make his mark on a woman; no matter his intentions. Research has shown that across all cultural boundaries, a straight man's visual cortex is designed to be attracted to an hourglass figure; a small waist, large breasts, flat stomach and full hips. A woman with these features tells his brain she is young and not pregnant, therefore making her desirable. This initial and very chemically driven urge and its degree of intensity is something that a woman cannot relate to even as she ogles at a hunky man. Her brain is wired to do something very different. She typically requires a tad more sensory input to evoke the type of sexual interest a man feels. At initial contact, a player may come across similarly to a man with virtuous intentions and this can be confusing to women.

A woman feels different emotions during sexual pursuit and subsequently they feel a different range of emotions when a relationship goes sour. Women also generally interpret sexual relationships differently in terms of how, why or when they go south. If she is not marred by drugs or alcohol addiction and her brain is functionally optimally, she will feel some form of hurt or abandonment when any sexual relationship ends no matter whether it was her fault or choice to end it. A man, on the other hand, has a greater capacity to separate sex from emotion; simply because he hasn't as many neural pathways from his emotional regions to the rest of his brain. This means he can more easily choose not to emotionally attach to his sex partners and therefore avoids some emotional pain. Females are more emotional because their brains are designed to attach feelings to just about everything they do. She therefore has a bigger fight to achieve "no strings attached" sexual encounters. There is no deficit in either sex. There are only differences. Either sex can achieve emotionally attached or detached sex but each has their respective level of difficulty. A woman however tends to interpret male detachment as something more threatening. He can enjoy a woman's company, conversation and body and then feel very little if she disappears from his life. A woman will miss any lover and if she feels she is not missed, it can disqualify the entire relationship because she can in no way relate to his indifference.

No matter a man's antics, whether he is the player or not, sexual pursuit is an establishment deeply rooted in his lifestyle. Whether mental or physical, he engages in sexual activity often. In one study, scientists scanned the brains of men and women having casual conversations at the office water cooler and found something very strange; to women that is. The male brains' sexual areas immediately activated as the conversations started; which means all the men saw these casual exchanges as an opportunity for sex. *All of them*; while the female brains did not apply any sexual regions; *like at all*. Interestingly, all the women merely saw the conversations as conversations. If you were to ask a woman her opinion of a man who thought he was going to get sex out of "Good morning, Fred. How are you?" she would likely call him an idiot. To women, this is creepy. To men, this is perfectly natural and normal. Both are correct. On a very basic level, finding him creepy helps her to narrow down mating selection. Accordingly, finding her sexually attractive helps ensure that our species procreates. It is crucial that a man is appropriate in what he does with this very innate instinct. When a man constantly prompts women for sex or if he never seeks a warm body, he fuses a "space of action" in his brain related to women, arousal, sex and orgasm. Either way, he must create an environment where he can safely maneuver through life as a sexual being.

The player has a range of schemes practiced in his neurons daily which control and manage his emotions. From his genes to social and cultural factors to the way he behaves around the women in his life; all have influenced the general way he views women by ingraining patterns in his brain. He grapples with forming a symbol of normalcy between his natural urges and his view and treatment of women. His behavioral patterns are a direct result of repetition and a culmination of his long-term emotional memory. He is used to the type and caliber of women and relationships he chooses. He is used to women leaving him after intervals of time. He is used to using charisma to acquire sexual encounters with multiple women. Finally, he is used to not caring for their emotional welfare and getting away with it. He has become accustomed to meticulously separating his sexual pursuits from his emotional affairs. An individual's neural pathways are designed to accommodate repetition so that the player is not in the neurological practice of commonly known aspects of loving relationships;

namely, kindness, sexual attentiveness and the willpower to delay your own gratification for the benefit of your mate. These are talents that must be practiced in order to perform them well.

EMPATHY

By definition, empathy is interpreting and relating to the feelings of others and also applies when understanding our own feelings. Cambridge University did a study specifically on how men and women respectively process empathy. The experiment involved roughly fifty men and fifty women who were administered various types of stimuli that were designed to gauge how well they could empathize. Scientists monitored the regional brain activity of each subject as they were asked to assess the needs and feelings of others. Then when asked to assess their own needs and feelings, the same regions of the brain lit up. This held true for both males and females but the study also found that, by volumes, females outperformed males on this task. The study proved that men have a harder time distinguishing distress and sadness on a human face whereas women show an almost sixth sense in this sport. More interestingly, males utilized a different brain strategy than females to process empathy. As a reminder, women become frustrated that men can't pull off this super power. This spells a real and deep perceptional difference between the sexes than cannot be ignored.

When a female pressures a male to empathize, it feels to him like he's being asked to perform magic and causes stress to his brain. To him it feels like the impossible. To her it feels like he has failed. I remember once being pissed because my husband had watched me drag a heavy glass coffee table clear across a room without offering to help. It turned out he was watching the game and hadn't even noticed that I was in the room. At the time I thought he was the dumbest person on the planet. Sometimes, depending on what his brain is doing, a man cannot be easily distracted much less can he stop to instantly empathize. Frustration is precisely what it feels like to a man when he is counted on to perform empathetic behaviors that certainly don't come naturally. An angry woman hollering on about "giving her a damned hand" can seem to come completely out of nowhere and he therefore feels disconnected with the insurmountable pressure of fixing something he can't fix. This is a concept that ties a man's brain in knots and he will likely give up. Without intending it, she is expecting him to read her mind. This is not to say that men cannot be empathic. They can but their brain has to be free from distraction because it is not as natural for him as it is for her. While a woman can smell heavy from a mile away, empathy is a tall order for a man. He's not an idiot for not noticing. His brain was likely busy doing something else and had blocked out anything that was not an urgent threat. Unless the glass coffee table was bucking or otherwise snarling and dangerous, most men won't get the same urgent cues as a female. A man in this position might defend, "If you need my help, all you have to do is ask," and regrettably for women, he's absolutely right.

Considering this, the player is certainly not in tune to empathize with his mark. His brain patterns are not well equipped to the type of self-control that is practiced in a mutually committed relationship. His neurology has in essence been trained to lie, ignore and justify when dealing with women.

He lies to, justifies about and ignores her emotional values because considering them causes him discomfort.

Men generally find it stressful to turn their emotions into words – that includes when they are talking to themselves and examining how they feel. On a functional MRI, when you have a conversation with yourself, your left temporal lobe lights up just as it would if you were speaking with someone else. A special region called the Wernickes area enables us to understand language, whether someone is speaking to us or whether we are interpreting our own thoughts. Forming words in our heads as we think things through is a process that can be difficult or stressful for males. In fact, men on average take seven hours longer than females to gain the ability to articulate how or why they feel emotional pain. Women can verbally assess a feeling almost instantly while a man may need a few days to work it out. Empathy requires this kind of internal articulation and assessment of feelings and since we know that practice makes perfect, one can easily deduce that a man who seeks to play women's' hearts is 100% out of practice when it comes to empathizing.

"NOTHING" IS REAL

A man's brain also needs rest. The female brain does not. This means while a woman thinks her lover is deeply contemplating some sound concept and asks, "What are you thinking about?" she should not be surprised if his reply is, "Nothing," because he really does mean it. There *is* such a thing, in fact if his brain didn't zone out and rest throughout his day and week, he would become a lunatic. Females can in no way relate to this phenomenon. There is not even a fleeting moment in her mental career where she spontaneously goes without naturally thinking about something, anything and everything; but never zoning off into *nothing*. A woman unaware of this male mental nothingness phenomenon may think he is either lying or just plain stupid if he claims to have nothing on his mind. Her brain is intertwined with neurological pathways which; barring intentional and deep yogic meditation, constantly create emotional values that she cannot escape, even for a millisecond. As women, think about the last time you heard yourself thinking, "What do you mean *nothing*? That's impossible. Liar!" This sentiment grossly outranks "lunatic" once you learn the science behind his super power to naturally stop and think about nothing. The concept of the "nothing stop", to females sounds like a "stupid stop" because females have no such stop.

It is no scientific mystery why men and women behave differently. We can't help it. Much of our behavior is prompted chemically and involuntarily. Our autonomic nervous system which handles involuntary action is always making suggestions while our somatic system, on the other hand, plays defense. As males and females, our offensive game is made up not only of a different team spirit and colors; we are also playing a different game and game strategy. There is no wonder in how things get a little confusing. The bottom line here is that in relationships, men typically perform up to whatever level they are required to; no more and no less. It is the female's job to choose which mate gets to hang around and which ones have to go. The trick is distinguishing between observing our lover's behaviors and interpreting them accurately. It would be nice if we had a definitive chart or index that would read our lover's actions (or lack thereof) and tell us what it all means. A website would be nice. This is why psychics and tarot card readers continue to make a decent living. An even less absurd approach would be to learn how hormones affect us so that you can recognize and separate "male" behavior from "player" behavior.

MALE NEUROHORMONES

Males and females utilize a different set of neurohormones to manage action and feeling which sometimes makes it tough for them to relate to one another. In relationships, men and women both have the tendency to project their standard of reasoning onto each other. He wants and expects her to think like him. Likewise, she expects him to see life from her perspective. Neither is possible. At best you can will yourself to do what you think the other expects, but you certainly can't think like them. Humans generally presume the world perceives as they do. All kinds of contentions evolve from this basic human flaw. He can no longer think like her than can the man on the moon. For the record, nobody lives on the moon.

Relationships end in bitterness and anger; all because of misunderstandings, hurt feelings and hopeless expectations. Understanding the physiological differences between the sexes can present clear explanations to these basic issues. Society leaves us at times indignant to the differences; asserting the battle of the sexes is offensive with males haughtily wielding testosterone and women flaunting all their frilly estrogen. The truth is, we should all be entitled to our own nature and recognizing its associated behaviors can not only take the pain out of ill relationships, it can keep them from reoccurring. Moreover, understanding hormones helps us erect healthy platforms on which to build a more pragmatic approach to intimacy.

TESTOSTERONE

Testosterone is the primary male sex hormone and is produced by the testicles in men and the ovaries in women. It is also produced in both sexes by the adrenal glands but in extremely low amounts in females. It is what makes human DNA *male*. In utero, it is responsible for molding the male reproduction system, masculinizes the brain and is essential for production of sperm in adult life. During adolescence, it deepens his voice, increases his penis size, forms hair all over his body and broadens his shoulders, jaw line and glabellum; the area between your eyebrows. After puberty, testosterone drives his sexual associations until he is dead. The hypothalamus and the pituitary glands in the brain are charged with regulating the amount of testosterone created by the testicles. During puberty, which starts between the ages of 9 and 14 (ending between ages 21 and 25), he is flooded with more testosterone than any other time in his life. After age 30, levels drop at a rate of about 1% each year.

Sexual arousal is initiated by the release of testosterone in males. First, desire causes the cerebral cortex to signal the hypothalamus which stimulates the testicles to produce testosterone. The frontal lobes don't chime in until the last few steps of arousal. This means, his brain and testicles react to a gorgeous woman before he does. Interestingly, production levels are limited by a "negative feedback loop" which is a checks and balances system in the brain so he doesn't create too much of the stuff. Testosterone persuades his mind at every turn and coupled with the hypothalamus; he certainly has one tall order if his mate expects him to only have eyes for her. In fact, it is damned near impossible and therefore a completely unrealistic expectation. He is designed to notice every woman that passes by, no matter what she looks like. His testicles and hypothalamus will work together to determine how attractive she is later. To women all over the globe; he can't help it. He has to notice other women. If he doesn't then he is probably noticing other men or he is excellent at hiding his wandering eye from you. If his testosterone levels are intact, he is definitely noticing somebody. It is normal. He is a sexual being so if a woman chooses to be angry that her love interest looks at other women, she should try not to be angry with him. She should try to be angry at testosterone as a whole. Or, a more realistic position would be to accept his design and not be offended that his brain is working optimally, whoever he's ogling at. Some might argue, "If he looks, he might touch." That's like saying if you walk into a bank and see the money, you might steal it. The cold truth is a man's wandering eye is not something a woman should take personally because it has nothing to do with her and everything to do with the simple fact that he is male. It is his wandering penis that she should be concerned with. A wondering eye is a reflex. A wondering penis however, is a frontal lobe choice.

VASOPRESSIN

Vasopressin has been esteemed as the "love" neurohormone in males. While this is true, it also regulates water in the body; working closely with the kidneys in both males and females and is therefore considered an antidiuretic hormone commonly known as arginine vasopressin hormone (ADH). When we feel dehydrated, vasopressin rushes into the bloodstream to retain and water and regulate sugar and salt levels in the blood. Vasopressin is produced by the posterior pituitary gland and although primarily released into the bloodstream, some amounts can be released directly into the brain which interestingly generate and maintain human social behaviors like pair bonding, sexual motivation and paternal responses to stress among others. It has a very short half-life at about 16 to 24 minutes which means unlike other social hormones, vasopressin spikes up as it increases then dips back down quickly. This hormone bounces on a line graph.

During its spike – in males usually during sex – vasopressin creates receptors in the brain which store a little bit of itself for later. While this happens, brain associations are made along with the other hormones that are simultaneously at play. If a man is having sex, his vasopressin (Vaso) will spike. If he is enjoying her either before, during or after the sex, his brain will also release his pleasure hormone, dopamine. When these two particular hormones fire at the same time in high levels, Vaso will deposit himself into receptors with a special note that reads something like, "So, this was totally good sex and we enjoyed this chick because Dopamine was out of control. Fun times indeed. Oh yeah! The chick's name is Cindy." At that stage, his brain will create a new chemical profile around Cindy. This profile can then be triggered when he hears her name, has a thought of her and most importantly when he is with her. If this process continues, over time, he will have deposited enough receptors and reserves of vasopressin with her name written all over it to increase his emotional value of her. This is the illustration of how men require time and repetition to fall in love. Once his brain attaches neural vasopressin, dopamine and a little oxytocin together enough times for the same woman, he falls in love and with men, once that profile is created, it almost never dissolves therefore, when men love they love deeply. The catch is, because of this intricate design; he can also very easily create multiple Vaso-profiles for each woman that he enjoys. He can develop a pocket for his wife, one for each of his lovers and a unique pocket of love for his favorite hooker. Good luck ladies.

OXYTOCIN

Oxytocin is produced deep inside the hypothalamus and released by the posterior pituitary. It is famous for being the human "pair bonding" hormone connecting humans in loving relationships. Release of this hormone occurs when we have sex, look into the eyes of our children or fall in love for example. Although both sexes utilize oxytocin for development of sexual reproduction before and after birth; in males, it is released at extremely low levels as compared to females. Women walk around experiencing oxytocin spikes all day; connecting objects and experiences with memories that flood their brains with bonding emotions while men generally experience the highest levels of oxytocin a few minutes after orgasm; also when his testosterone levels are lowest. Men therefore bond in a different way than women. Oxytocin is not a major player when a man is falling in love but is absolutely necessary for women to feel love. Knowing this is integral as women try to relate to their lovers. He certainly loves and in fact, the neural evidence of his love emotion lays a deeper and more permanent imprint on this brain than a female's. It just feels different and takes much longer to develop.

THE FEMALE BRAIN

There is a whole lot of "crazy" that can be explained inside the female brain. Because of the complex levels of emotional involvement within its functions, it is a completely different animal than the male brain. For example, women have approximately 30% more neural pathways connected between emotive and verbal centers. The implication here is that it is imperative for a woman to talk her feelings out. She is not strange or odd because she needs to talk. She's wired to communicate and needs to verbalize in order to process stress effectively. Her supermarket trip, her best friend, her hangnail; everything qualifies if it made her feel some kind of way. Damned near everything a woman experiences creates an emotional response. A man's emotional triggers, however, are in many ways linked to muscle which is why driving fast, moving a basketball or sex often helps men relieve stress rather than talking or connecting with people. Men need silence, space and the ability to move a ball or their bodies around. Take this away from him and he's not a happy camper.

Remove a woman's ability to express her emotions and you'll really know crazy. Inside the female brain, emotional chemistry sets her apart as she serves the great purpose of coddling the harsh world around her. Some call it crazy. I call it versatility. She is the guru on the production and handling of all ranges of emotive response.

WOMEN ARE DIFFERENT, NOT CRAZY

The female remains a great mystery to all, including those who are female. As a female, this is sometimes embarrassing. Nonetheless, the woman is quite a philosophical creature. To try and explain her away without becoming philosophical would be absurd. I'll give you a strong philosophical foundation of the female's role and purpose just to give you somewhere to land all the female hormonal stuff we'll get into later. I hope I have your attention, in fact I suppose a few of you couldn't resist the temptation to open this book and start reading at this chapter. Here goes nothing!

People often consider unexplained behavior to be unfavorable. If someone exhibits behavior that you cannot understand, you perceive it as strange or even insane as long as the meaning behind the behavior remains a mystery. In some cases, if you can get the back-story and gain an understanding, the behavior can become interesting or even fascinating. For example, a genius that can do complicated math in his head without a calculator may require a strange tilt of the neck as he thinks. From a far, he may look insane doing this. Once you learn of his genius, you might go home and try the head tilt yourself to see if it helps you figure out some household calculation; suddenly impressed with what you originally thought was insane. The purpose of this section is to explain that female behavior, just like all behavior, is a result of a chemical reaction and hers, although strange and mysterious, is one that is necessary for the survival of mankind.

I propose men have generally viewed women as odd since the beginning of time yet they are equally valued as important nurturers and the givers of life; the help-mate to other men, women and children. The old adage, "Women… can't live with 'em; can't live without 'em," holds some scientific weight. Nature seems to create a natural phenomenon of checks and balances that can require a constant tug and pull, pain for gain, love for loss or any otherwise exchange of negative and positive energies; like electricity for example. Without getting too theoretical nature has a dirty little way of causing us great misfortune before fortune and vice versa with constant cyclical loops of history, ideologies, habits, hurts and joys. No new problems are invented. We seem to suffer the same sets of challenges in different forms all over the planet, time and time again. With the female, hers is a negation of welfare; hers versus the world's. When she matures through her servitude she can learn to commit to her own welfare. While she navigates the welfare of others however, often she must fully forsake herself.

The female is the life-giver; full of mysterious strength, wisdom and human insight but full of contradictions, always changing her mind; seemingly emotionally unstable. How could this most valuable creature simultaneously be insane? She is in fact, not insane. She is different than men and her differences are what make her particular strengths possible. To endure the biological and hormonal changes involved in carrying and birthing offspring, to be wives to men and mothers to all and to nurture the world with caring comforts and the figurative "tucking in" of people; all require a great emotional capacity. She seems to be designed to care for everyone and serve the world. For example, the female is chemically designed to do amazingly better than men at reading people's facial expressions and observing emotions in others simply because her hippocampus is larger. This also explains why she can on average remember more details of emotional events than he can. In the area of communicating through language and hearing, she possesses on average about 11% more neurons to assist her. It is therefore no mystery why, although completely necessary, feminine emotion has been forever misconstrued as insanity. It is simply because men, in a male-centered world, cannot make heads or tails of this very emotional creature called the female.

EMOTIONAL GLUE

The truth is, since women have more neural pathways connecting to emotive centers, women attach emotions to everything they experience. Everything is emotional – which is normal to her – but men cannot relate to this continual "caring" about everything so when she shows emotional attachment to everyday objects and situations, it looks crazy to him. If she is much more or less excited, saddened or emotionally reactive to something that does not affect him, he cannot understand or relate. "She's overreacting," he concludes. Effective reasoning however, is in her neurohormones; not his perspective of her. She can't help feeling any more than he can help not feeling. Her brain is structured in a way that makes it perfectly possible for her to care about and notice everything. If this is insanity, it is a necessary one.

She is the emotional glue for the world. Imagine a world where women were not emotional. Who would help folks through their emotional pain? Who would thoughtfully care for and nurture the children of the world? Who would have figured out that when you need a band aid, you also need a hug? Who would be sure to change your diaper or feed you because you were crying? Who else would have gotten angry because you forgot to close the refrigerator? Subsequently, how would you have learned the importance of saving electricity, being polite to others, being careful, cleaning your bottom and wiping your nose? Who would have taught you how to cope with negative feelings and be emotionally healthy? Emotional women are an important part of the survival of society just as males, being less emotional, also serve their respective purpose along with children, elephants and sugar canes. Everything that was created is therefore necessary, including female emotions.

TRIGGERS

Simply put, our brain's response to emotional stress is a mechanism designed to protect us from dangers in the wild. While we no longer live in the wild, as women, our daily perception of danger lies in the balancing of work, school, family and the rigorous pressure to keep up with it all while looking like a lady. To a woman, a past due bill can trigger a type of stress that tells her imminent danger is near as the survival of herself and family are in jeopardy. Men on the other hand, don't react the same way. A past due bill is a not a trigger to his danger centers. Typically, his danger receptors require a more physical type of danger. The past due bill would have to grow arms, legs and begin attacking for him to appear concerned. In short, male and females do not share the same sets of stress triggers so trying to relate in this area is difficult. One is usually perceived as either under or overreacting.

My ex-husband and I had a terrible argument when he took over the grocery shopping one week. When he got to the toilet paper isle, he decided to buy a different brand because it was on sale. Unbeknownst to him, toilet paper can be very emotionally connected for women. Some of us can't just wipe ourselves down there with just anything. I have a favorite kind that reacts with my privates in a certain kind of way. Sale or full price, I needed my Charmin so we defended our cases. I wanted my toilet paper and general control of my nest. He wanted appreciation for making a good financial decision. It felt offensive that he stood this ground. What? Am I just supposed to walk around with toilet paper stuck to my ass so he can feel like a man? He didn't care what kind of paper we used. He just wanted me to respect his decision. I certainly cared what paper we used and I also wanted him to respect my decision. He thought I was making a big deal and I thought the same of him. He was upset that I was upset and vice versa. Eventually this power struggle ended us with two types of toilet paper, toothpaste, soap and shampoo in the house. I doubt it had anything to do with brand names. I knew he had not picked this fight but I couldn't understand why he wouldn't automatically concede. It hurt. I became emotional and so did he. "I just want to wipe my butt with same paper I've been using for 10 years," I thought to myself while actually crying. Of course, he wasn't seeing it the same way and did not understand the emotional piece at all. All he knew was that I was crying over toilet paper. I was actually crying over a failure to connect with my husband.

What had started as a small battle over jurisdiction had turned into what to me felt like more gut-wrenching evidence of our failure as a couple. The bottom line was that we could not effectively communicate, no matter whether we were talking sex, kids or toilet paper. It was hopeless and yet I didn't give in. I went out and spitefully bought the toilet paper I wanted. Suddenly, the Charmin logo became a marker of contention in our marriage. Shame on us. Sure, I could have picked my battles better. I could have just sucked it up until it was my turn to grocery shop. At any rate, he thought I was crazy as hell for being so offended. One feeling had led to another and my amygdala reacted. I was devastated that we couldn't get anything right together. Was I crazy? No. Did I overreact? Possibly. Did he overreact? Perhaps. The point is it wasn't about the paper. Our marriage was actually failing and the fact that we were fighting about toilet paper made that real to me so I cried. I wasn't being crazy; I was being emotional because my Spidey senses could tell our new marriage was pretty much over. The paper was a danger cue.

SENSITIVITY

It may be an untold secret that many mature women believe men are more sensitive creatures and that females are pegged wrongly as more sensitive merely because they are emotional more often. When men become emotional, they "turn into big babies," at least this is the typical remark from women. Who is more emotional? Clearly women are. Who is more sensitive? I dare suffer the reaction of males cringing when I assert that clearly, men are. (There, I said it.) No one can disagree that men are less emotional because proof is in the neurons. Here is my simple point. It is then also true that men do not have as much experience at being emotional. No matter how you cut it, practice makes perfect and when men become emotional, they feel like a fish out of water and their feelings run deep as the water itself. Men are not experts at being emotional. Therefore, they alternate between avoiding and overreacting to their feelings and when men are sad, they are some kinda sad, honey! And when they're sick, forget about it. Somebody's got another baby to care for. Even little boys get all crazy when they don't get their way compared to little girls. Their tantrums may be less frequent than females but they are more severe. As adults, these episodes are steeped in his ego. We walk on eggshells around the men in our lives because we know their threshold to handle the truth is less than ours and thereby, we avoid grown man tantrums. Men are the more sensitive sex. This is a known fact and also something women "shush" at because we know better than to announce it a loud. We whisper to our daughters about it being true. I shall not argue any further.

FEMALE NEUROHORMONES

A slew of hormones control development and emotional maintenance of the female body. In utero, this party of players set a completely different course for develop that shape not only the body into "female" but also her emotions and the way she experiences life. These include estrogen, oxytocin, progesterone, testosterone, cortisol, vasopressin, DHEA and androstenedione.

ESTROGEN

Estrogen is the main player in making a person female and is produced mainly by the ovaries. The presence of this hormone channels the development of female characteristics. Male to female transgendered successfully use types of estrogen to reframe their bodies into a more feminine shape. The effects of these synthetic forms of estrogen in high doses can transform a man's face and body to resemble a woman's quite impressively, especially if administration begins during adolescence or before puberty begins. Thailand is famous for its lady boy population, in part due to the availability of contraceptives. In Thailand you don't need a prescription to buy medication. You can buy just about anything over the counter so many self-administer the estrogen found in birth control pills at early ages to thwart the natural effects of testosterone and develop very feminine physical bodies; including thinner waists, a less pronounced laryngeal prominence (Adam's apple), higher pitched voices and the growth of breasts. Very many Thai transgendered women look and even sound so feminine; barring a glimpse at their male genitals, most people could not differentiate them as having been born male.

Estrogen *or oestrogen* is a sex hormone which means it configures biological sex makeup. Oestrogen (an estrogen) is one of three of these types of hormones; the other two being testosterone (an androgen) and progesterone (a progestogen that we'll cover in the next section). Androgens like testosterone are usually steroid hormones defined by their stimulation and control of the development and maintenance of male characteristics in the vertebrates. These build the body up to a deeper voice, broader shoulders and increased facial bone structure. Estrogens, on the other hand cause feminine attributes affecting more fat to deposit along the hips, buttocks and thighs, lowered bone mass in the jaws, shoulders and glabellum. These physical attributes are considered female secondary sexual characteristics while primary sexual characteristics include development of the female reproductive system. Interestingly, while estrogen is considered the "female" hormone, males maintain very low levels of it during adolescent development. After puberty and gradually with age, estrogen levels increase in males.

In regard to levels of estrogen and its effect on our psychology, research is rudimentary at best. Scientists know estrogen has a wide range of effects on the body and brain. It operates within the central nervous system through very complex networks that affect our physiology and psychology. It lends an enormous hand in the creation and efficiency of neurotransmitters in the amygdala, hippocampus and prefrontal lobes which are the brain regions related to emotion and cognition. Most notably, estrogen can also affect the intensity of emotional experiences however, since emotional intensity is not something that can yet be measured, the science in this area has much room to expand.

Defining the specific relationship between psychology and estrogen is problematic due to the fact that estrogen works together with other chemicals in multiple systems in the body to effect emotional change. Estrogen replacement therapy is often used in postmenopausal women to improve mood and energy levels yet studies have also reported that it can cause fear and anxiety; therefore, the impact of estrogen on emotion varies and may depend on the individual's current state and the situation. Therefore, how estrogen affects a woman's psychology will depends on her chemical makeup and how the separate pieces to her "estrogen systems" congregate. [In application, if you're already all jacked up in love with somebody who you know to be a player, your estrogen may have a different effect on you this year than last year. Presumably, the same difference would apply the following year once you're finally over the guy.] We have yet to achieve a comprehensive understanding of the neurological, psychological and physiological relationships between estrogen and emotional changes. Once we do, it will lead to promising and more effective treatment for female emotional disorders.

OXYTOCIN

Of all the hormones that affect a woman's emotional value of others, oxytocin is certainly the most influential. It is known as the "love" or "bonding" hormone and it does just that; essentially aiding women in the aiding of others; her children, her pets, her parents, her plants and of course her lover. Oxytocin is normally produced by the emotional hypothalamus and then released by the pituitary and is involved in sexual reproductive development before and after birth in both sexes. It is typically released in response to the stretching of the cervix and uterus during childbirth and stimulation of the nipples, especially during breastfeeding. It also plays a huge role during and after sexual encounters in both males and females causing them to have loving "feelings" towards their sex partner. As mentioned, vasopressin is the closest hormonal equivalent in the male who typically carries extremely low levels of oxytocin; in fact, his highest spike of oxytocin occurs just a few minutes after he has an orgasm; which explains why some men are barely interested in cuddling any other time. Females on the other hand, walk around throughout their days experiencing moderate bursts of oxytocin. Naturally, this facilitates her as the nurturer *or gatherer* and emotional comforter to the world. By design, this helps our survival as a species just as male testosterone thwarts oxytocin and other emotional hormones so he can endure with a sense of bravery being *the hunter*; exhibiting great strength and protection to the world. The eco-system has left no stone uncovered and every single piece to life's design points inevitably to our survival. Everything we are is necessary. The male and the female are equally as important to the earth.

When a woman has sex, oxytocin is fired in high doses. If she is enjoying the feeling her partner is giving her, dopamine will also fire in high doses; especially if she reaches orgasm. These two fire enough times together with the same guy and she's in love. Simple as that and it can even happen on the first sexual encounter. If she feels good enough with him that first time – relative to all the other emotional triggers in life – she can fall head over heels in love with the complete stranger. With men, you'll remember a much more complicated and planned out route to the feeling of being in love which requires sex and pleasure over time and with much repetition.

With females, however, it's a pretty short and straight shot. Simply mix a little accelerated levels of oxytocin with dopamine and she can feel like love out the gate. While men have a ping pong match with vasopressin spiking and dropping over time; whose bursts gradually lead him to affectionate feelings, the female's oxytocin-dopamine cocktail moves her in one fierce and constant direction towards love. The force can feel unstoppable. If she is a mature woman, she will recognize and understand this emotional rush as a warning to be cautious and not rush into every relationship that makes her feel good.

Oxytocin is the main female player that solidifies the realization that she has found a lover in whom she trusts. The evidence of this trust lies in her ability to orgasm while either being touched by or thinking of her love interest. Her orgasm is not primarily physiological but a combination of emotional and biological factors. If she can actually achieve orgasm from being touched by her lover, it means she not only trusts, enjoys and is attracted to him or her, it also means this other person is in tune with her body and understands the emotional and physiological techniques that give her pleasure. This for females is rare, valuable and highly coveted. To the female, mutual love seems the most obvious excuse for such pleasure. Oxytocin plays an integral role in a woman's love associations of all kinds.

PROGESTERONE

Females need progesterone in order to reproduce offspring among other things. It is a steroid and sex hormone that is involved in menstruation, pregnancy and embryogenesis in humans and other species. Progesterone also enhances the function of serotonin receptors so excess and deficits of this stuff can result in neurochemical issues. As progesterone drops below relative levels, a deficit in serotonin can occur. Serotonin is closely related to frontal lobe dopamine systems which control the level of pleasure you can feel. Low progesterone levels mean these women find it more difficult to feel pleasure. Low serotonin is also linked to pleasure seeking behaviors like smoking cigarettes and drinking alcohol.

CORTISOL

Cortisol is the hormone released in both sexes to administer a sense of stress or urgency. Your body floods with cortisol to help you focus on solutions to danger and facilitate survival. Scientists have observed a particular negative correlation between memory and stress which suggests people typically have a hard time recalling memories that occurred during or just before stressful events. Interestingly, when you look deeper into the study, you'll find it generally holds true for men, not so much for women. Cortisol seems to make a positive influence on female memory, a hugely negative impact on male memory and no one knows why or how. (Wolf, Schommer, Hellhammer, McEwen, Kirschbaum., 2011)

CHAPTER 4 | THE SEX OF THE GAME

There are many differences between the sexes; the most significant is
sex no matter how you slice it.

Figuring you would be exhausted by now, I've strategically placed this sex chapter following the biology chapter to cut you a break. Well done, by the way. This short chapter shall be your reward.

What is sex? By definition, it is the physical process of combining male and female genes to form offspring. Sexual desire can be defined as the drive that motivates individuals to fantasize about or seek out sexual activity. Sexual arousal on the other hand is defined as the "autonomic physiological processes" that prepare the mind and body for sexual encounters. (Pfaus., 2009) In other words, arousal is a biological response to stimulus. Boy see girl. Boy's body likes girl. Boy now likes girl. The same applies for women. Your brain knows what you like when you see it, smell it, taste it, hear it or touch it; even before you do. Sexual arousal happens without your control and causes additional physiological phenomena including an increased heart rate and mucho saliva. It is important that a clear distinction be made between these terms. Sex, sexual desire and sexual arousal are all of what we're talking about in this chapter. All three after all, are a huge part of falling in love, falling out of love and generally being human. The goal in this chapter is to give you an understanding of how sex, sexual desire and arousal all coil up together to make you feel amazing and can sometimes masquerade as feelings of love and connectedness; especially for women. It's certainly okay to have sex, desire and arousal; all at the same time. The tricky part is not allowing all that dopamine to convince you that you've met the love of your life. Sometimes, all it really means is that you've had some decent sex.

While you may be beating yourself up for having been played or perhaps, you're the player, feeling proud of yourself; keep in mind that the biology of sex goes hand in hand with the psychology of it. A large part of all the decisions you played a part in that culminated to the codependent relationship that developed, came about due to your psychology or your way of thinking about him or her. If you'll recall, your psychology is a direct result of your interaction with your chemical or hormonal balances. Emotions and chemicals do a delicate binary dance with each other. At times, each can take control but ultimately neither dictates the other. Our minds and bodies are too rigged up full of trip wires and checks and balances. The important thing to remember is that you are in fact in a battle for your senses. It's you against your chemicals; especially when it comes to sex. From a chemical standpoint, besides having a baby, no other natural bodily function is a more formidable opponent against your sound mind than sexual activity's effect on your hormonal balance. The implication then is that the question isn't what the sex is doing to you, it becomes more about who you are deciding to give your sexual energy to and why.

GOOD VS. BAD SEX

I'll be plain here. Just because something feels good doesn't mean it is good. We all know it because we've heard it a thousand times. In fact, I'm guessing that smoking crack feels remarkable. But don't you remember? Crack is wack and yet people try it for the first time because they want to experience a good feeling. For that matter, good sex with the wrong person isn't actually *good sex*. It's the final outcome that we're gauging here. One can have amazing sex then subsequently walk away with a slew of problems including and not limited to; herpes, an unwanted pregnancy or a broken heart.

Women have to be especially careful when balancing sexual pleasure with a man that is treating her poorly. Tons of emotional neural attachments are formed during sex for both men and women but some of the females' are much deeper. Scientists found that lust outright overpowers feelings of disgust in women but not so much in men. One experiment exposed women to different types of stimulation; one being, sexually erotic videos geared towards women. After the exposure, these female groups were all asked to perform disgusting tasks which included drinking from a cup that may have had an insect in it, wiping their hands with a presumably used tissue and placing their finger into a container of condoms that were apparently used. The women who had moments ago been exposed to sexually arousing videos were more willing to perform these tasks than the other groups. Notably, the other groups were exposed to different stimulus which included boring informational videos while another group watched exhilarating extreme sports sequences. What this implies is that when a woman is sexually aroused, she may be more accepting of her partners' disgusting habits; aka his bad behavior.

When I was with my player, I felt amazing. Everything was good. Nothing was bad. I always woke up feeling refreshed and happy, then right around noon my gut would start to catch up to itself. By supper it was back to reality and I knew in my gut, head and heart that I was in an emotionally toxic situation. Any sexual pleasure I was getting from him physically was not a help to me mentally. Good sex, therefore, is any sex you enjoy that you don't feel bad about later. If your player is making you orgasm up the walls, count your blessings, cut your losses and get out of the kitchen unless you enjoy being emotionally baked to death.

What the mark must also bear in mind is that emotional feelings will alter and often amplify physical pleasures from sex. If a stranger grabs your shoulder it feels icky but if your crush does it, it takes your breath away. Sex too feels way better when you know and care for the other person. If the mark has fallen or is falling in love, sex can feel amazing no matter how her player touches her. In some cases, the player will turn the sex strategy into a game of pleasing him; constantly coaching and coaxing his mark to obsess over his body instead of focusing any attention on her. She is then only allowed to gain pleasure from giving him pleasure.

On the other hand, some players are very skilled lovers and know that great sex – to any woman in love – is a force that cannot be reckoned with. Her emotional feelings plus his amazing sex will cause her heart and brain to conspire against her and she'll be hooked leaving him no need to seek her out ever again. She will forever be the one to initiate contact and chase his attention. Sadly, her main form of enticement becomes sexual activity because sex has become the only way she is allowed to connect with him. In this position, he can spend more or less energy on her as the relationship becomes automatic. Her only defense against this type of emotional imprisonment is to refrain from sexual interactions with her player. The connection is undeniable. If a woman has fallen in love with a player, her emotional stability depends on her sexual detachment from him; period.

FANTASY VS. NEURAL FUNCTION

Fantasy is a powerful platform in every person's life. Fantasizing affects your emotional levels, makes you zealous and drives you towards your obsessions; good or bad. Without it, we would never visualize our goals. If Fred Astaire had never fantasized about becoming a dancer, he would have never tapped his foot once and his genius would have remained hidden from the world. We fantasize about everything from career goals to winning the lottery, future spouses and even solving world hunger. Therefore, everyone uses fantasy of some sort. Sexual fantasy, however, is perhaps the most popular. Yet, the female; being a peculiar creature, is quite the romantic dreamer. Because the female orgasm is so emotionally linked, she sometimes masturbates to images of passionate sex chopped full of emotions and mutual feelings. This can have a devastating effect on her sense of reality; especially if she is in love with someone that doesn't love her.

There came a point where I realized that I could not think about sex with someone else. My player was all my brain wanted. He had been the only man I had fantasized about for over a year; every night without fail. My pleasure centers had a sure shot series of "go-to" fantasies and every single one of them revolved around him. One night, I tried to fantasize about another man but failed to reach orgasm. The next night, I tried again and still, my player popped into my fantasy as soon as it got hot and he took me to orgasm. After a week of this nonsense, I realized I had a big problem. It wasn't quite an "Ah ha!" moment. It was more like, "Oh fuck!" I realized that I could not successfully orgasm without thinking of him. Realizing that felt dangerous as hell. Never, and I mean never in my life had I wound up in such a predicament. Suddenly, it occurred to me that he had been the first man I had fallen in love with sober; full of raw, unalcohol-treated emotions. *Ouch!* It felt deep however; I shelved that concept and kept on moving forward. Soon I discovered the test of reversing the damage I had done had created a phenomenal challenge, what with all my unrestrained, unalcohol-treated fantasizing and all.

No matter how hard I tried, no other image aroused me more than his. It was terrifying only because I knew he didn't love me. It was hopeless because I knew I would never be in his life in any serious capacity yet carelessly, in each one of my fantasies we were making love in our way; the way we engaged. The difference was that I padded my fantasies with emotion; his and mine. It wasn't just the sex images that were getting me off. I was especially turned on by the love feelings, connectedness and mutual respect I was attaching to the imagery. My deepest fantasy was that he was secretly in love with me. This made the sexual images and feelings much more powerful and it gave me great pleasure. Thinking about another man felt like cheating.

I'm a savage in my fantasy life because of my extremely vivid imagination and I thought of all kinds of scenarios and situations that I had no confidence were even possible in real life. I didn't hold back and it was quite racy and played all kind of tricks on my neurochemistry. I had etched a damned near permanent and fully devoted sexual pathway centered on and steeped in him. What an idiot move. It seemed impermeable because at the end of it all, I'm human. I enjoyed it; point blank. I loved it. Just like two-thirds of the world, I'm calling the "addictive personality" card. I loved thinking about the two of us naked. I absolutely loved the way being with him seemed to temporarily put me back together. At one point I referred to him as my "dopamine fix" which couldn't have been more accurate. In reality, he didn't treat me special and my entire concept of his character had been a theoretical construct; merely based on a true story. It was foolish and I knew I had to figure out how to escape its power. Once I began to formulate my exit strategy and get him out of my mind, my first plan of action was to stop masturbating. There was no middle ground. I couldn't be attracted to anyone else. Every other man looked like a boy to me so instead of replacing him, I went cold-turkey and stopped being sexual for a time. Man was that tough. But boy did it work.

The brain contains an estimated thirty regions that process visual imagery, most of which reside in the temporal lobes. There are two basic pathways that images follow in order for them to dance around in our heads in a way we can process, recall, analyze and enjoy them. If the image is of something tangible that is within our optical vision, this pathway starts with the eyes. When we are looking at a real object, signals travel through the eyes, clear through the middle of the brain, all the way to the back of the occipital lobe where the "whats" and "hows" get answered. We immediately assess an answer to "What is it?" and "How is it situated?" Once the occipital makes sense of what we're looking at, signals travel to the top of the brain where more "hows" get answered in the parietal lobes. We must answer questions like, "Is it dangerous?" or "Will it give us a reward?" which trigger movement to emotional centers and the party begins in the temporal and limbic regions.

Let's assume this process looks like a figure eight, loopty-loop on a functional MRI. Like a go-cart traveling around the track, your loop starts with the eyes and continues until the real-life experience is over. On the other hand, if your images are coming from you; that is, if you are fantasizing a new scenario or remembering an old flame, that loopty-loop still happens; it just happens in reverse. The same chemical pathways activate as if you were seeing the image with your eyes, so although you can tell the difference between fantasy and reality; separately, certain regions of your brain, your physical body and your emotional responses cannot. Be then careful about how you fantasize because this process also explains why a person, after telling the same lie again and again, can begin to believe it as truth. Eventually, fantasy can feel real and the more you engage in unrealistic love fantasy, the further you dive into an emotional and neurological rabbit hole.

BLOWJOBS VS. INTERCOURSE

Choose wisely. I chose blow jobs and still ended up broken hearted. My player and I didn't regularly have intercourse and I liked it that way because instinctively, I was terrified that if we had, I would have fallen even deeper in love. Intercourse is certainly very connecting and emotional for the female however, according to my calculations, so are blowjobs. The problem with most women is that fantasy is where she entertains all her hopes of mutual love. Whether she is engaging in intercourse, oral or strictly hand jobs; in her mind, she is likely making love.

In application, deciding on whether to administer blowjobs or vagina is like an alcoholic deciding between beer and wine. Either way, you're going to end up getting drunk. Blowjobs, hand jobs, intercourse, anal, voyeurism, mutual masturbation, kissing or whatever else you decide on; if you are falling for someone who is using you for your body parts, you're in trouble. Safely, the question then isn't between your upper and lower levels, it is more appropriate that we can settle on the term *sexual activity* which appropriately includes "all of the above". This implies that it doesn't matter what types of sexual activity; *should* you choose, you are agreeing to share an intimate moment with someone who devalues you.

CHAPTER 5 | THE SIGNS OF THE GAME

If a creature neglects the world and considers only itself, it becomes a highly dangerous mechanism.

If you are a woman discovering your emotions have been played, you've undoubtedly sorted through endless Internet searches, peeled through countless articles on identifying the signs of a player, read books and agonized over conversations with your girlfriends; anything to help you understand how you got caught up in this mess. Searching for clarity in her emotional values is a woman's only resource when her heart is torn into two. One side pits against the other. The first urges her to stay in a questionable relationship and the second pushes her away. To settle in the middle can be a terrible place to live yet tolerating the unbalanced pain to pleasure ratio is where women are experts because this is a place in life, she inadvertently finds herself often.

She continually looks for evidence that the world appreciates her. A woman in love hopes to find positive clues; that is, evidence of her lover's compassion. Trouble is you can't intellectually finagle your way out of an emotional mess. Albeit, we all attempt this impossible feat; to reason with our emotions, strategically picking the figurative rose with, "He loves me.

He loves me not." Now stop. Hammer time. It's insanity. If it doesn't feel right, he probably loves you not. When a man loves a woman, she knows it.

The important thing to remember here is that your perception of the raw input you take from the world through sight, sound, taste, touch and smell all shape how you interpret your surroundings. In other words, all you have are the lenses through which life is observed. Further, your state of emotions and surroundings contribute to a great degree how that lens is shaped and positioned. He may love you. He may not. Whether he loves you or not isn't the issue. The issue is whether you value your perspective enough to evaluate how you feel. The question is, "Does *your* love have a contingency?" Your perspective is the one you have to deal with, not his. If your current situation is working for you, then you don't have a problem. You only have a problem if some component of what you are experiencing is not working. What I'm getting at here is that your "player checklist" is in your own perspective. Yours depends on you and how you perceive the man you love. Therefore, the only feasible item on your checklist should be an answer to, "What am I willing to put up with?"

To interpret this section as a guideline to determine if the man in your life is a player would be to minimize the complexity of mankind. To infer that you can categorize, set apart or otherwise identify a type of human through a list of characteristics is a slippery slope, one that Adolf Hitler certainly exhausted thoroughly and never carefully. I can no more create a guideline of psychological characteristics of what definitively qualifies a man to be a "complete player" than Adolf Hitler could have asserted his case for what the perfect human should look like. I can however, point out some common situations that might be interpreted as behavioral "red flags".

As with symptoms of disease, typically characteristics congregate. A people suffering from the same disease often share a slew of common symptoms. This makes the picking apart of individual characteristics less important than the tethering of the totality of their behaviors. This is also how you get a full picture of a person's face. Your brain will recognize each part of a person's face then congregate the details together so that you see their face as a whole object. In fact, there is a specific part of the brain that is dedicated to recognizing human faces. (Interestingly, a different part of the brain is used to recognize cartoons faces.) To cue in on a person's nose or upper lip would take more concentration and utilizes a different area of the brain. The brain understands the importance of recognizing a person based on the totality of their facial characteristics, not the individual parts. Your goal in this section should not be to count how many of these signs apply to the man you love. At best, try to better understand the summation of his personality and the value he places on your relationship.

Initially, when I started my journey to understand my heartbreak, I didn't know what I would find but I was hopeful to find an answer; any answer. At first, I Google searched all the usual headlines, "Is he in love or faking?" and "How to know when the relationship is over." I was looking for a checklist. I felt like I needed a guideline of clues to help me decide whether my lover was good or evil. I assumed that there were some common denominators but I found no such list. In reality, when scientists study psychology, they don't end up with checklists either. They end up with highly complicated math algorithms and fair to poorly written theories and theses, scatter charts – and all types of charts – and they apply statistical math to find correlations between numbers of variables, cross cultural factors and so on and yadda yadda. It is a highly complicated process to study behavior and cannot be narrowed down to any magical list. Beware of tabloid media which are full of strange associations and inference but have no roots in science. These are easy, misrouted educational resources for folks who really don't care to know the truth.

Whether your lover matches all, most, few or none of the items on this list, read carefully and go with your gut. There is no score card. Your job is to get to the end of the list and feel more confident about the very important decision you'll make. In the famous words of The Clash, "Should I Stay or Should I Go?"

Boil down your possibilities and make a decision on where to draw boundaries based on your relationship. No one can know the depth or lack of intimacy that you and your lover share. Equally true; no one can know the type of toxic despair you both consume together. Cut your losses now if you have to. The earlier you get out the better if you can't stomach the relationship. Otherwise, hold on tight and take the risk at continuing to love him. Eventually you will come know the truth about how he feels. Only you can make the assessment because even if you ask, you cannot be sure he will tell the truth. Life never goes without its share of risks and failures so pick the meat from the bones and purely discern your perspective (not his) and you will remain blameless no matter your choice.

THE AMBIGUOUS CHECKLIST

Firstly, your gut is your best friend. Trust it. If you feel you are in a one-sided relationship, you probably are. It may hurt to step away from someone you love but if you are in love with someone who does not have your best interest at heart, it already hurts and the pain is getting worse. Your best course of action is to step away at least for a time so you and your gut can have a more clear conversation.

✓ A player may come on strong in the very beginning and make you think he's chosen you for a possible life mate. For example, he may allude to you being "wife material" or suggest he talked to a close friend or relative about you. If this happens quickly, within the first few days or weeks, it is a sign to be cautious. Sincere expressions of love and hope of a long-term relationship out the gate are not indicative of typical male behavior. Be careful.

✓ The player has the perfect excuse for never inviting you to his home. "It's filthy," is a fairly typical exemption. He knows better than to ever let you know where he lives because you might be the type that key cars or shows up unannounced. If he is okay with letting you know where he lives, he may only allow your entrance and exit at night.

✓ A player knows to ask you specific questions about your experiences especially within the first few weeks of your romantic relationship. He does this so you feel connected with him. Sharing personal stories cues a woman's brain to fire oxytocin which emotionally bonds her to the person she is with. He will make a note to ask you about something you said in a previous conversation. This makes you think he is listening and cares about your life. This type of attention is normal for a man with long-term intentions, however, if it does not remain consistent, beware. If he's interested in you, it will be continual and should not wane after the first few weeks or months of the relationship.

✓ When asked about his past relationships, the player's answer to why the relationship ended is almost always, "She was crazy." He will give no further explanation. Remember, there are always two sides to a story and a man with no intention of developing feelings will avoid answering questions that relate to past relationships. He also may not have given the time to consider the reasons the relationship ended and therefore may not know the answer.

✓ You have to reach him in order to stay on his radar. This is in some way to keep you desperate but it may also be because he cannot keep track of when he's last contacted his marks. He confidently relies on the women in his life to maintain frequency of communication. He knows they will always seek him out if he has forgotten them. A man who is truly interested in a woman will initiate contact with her.

✓ He may avoid eye contact after he becomes aware she is in love. If he is aware she is in love, he may withhold his gaze; knowing that direct eye contact is a principle part of intimate connectivity. If he is not in love, engaging in eye to eye contact with someone who is in love feels awkward.

✓ He may confuse his marks accidently referring to them by the wrong name or confuse events placing himself in memory with the wrong participant. While it is fairly normal for both men and women to occasionally mistake a party member from a memory, if it occurs regularly, it may indicate you are one of many women in his life.

✓ He may coerce his mark to engage in sexual practices even if she shows a clear disinterest. If you feel pressured to perform any sexual act that you don't want to and have clearly expressed disgust for, there is something deeply troubling about the person doing the pressuring. Get away as soon as possible.

✓ He may become amused by your pain; that is, if he takes an action to hurt your feelings then boasts, brags or laughs about it. If he uses hurtful words to make you cry then teases you for being weak, his interest is not yours and you should reevaluate the way you value his interaction in your life. Men also tend to laugh when they are not sure how to answer a question so be careful not to confuse his nervousness with cruelty.

✓ Lastly, if your love interest does not take you on dates or make an effort to spend time with you outside of the bedroom, there is a problem. When a man is interested in the whole woman, he will engage in non-sex related activities with her. The mark may feel that the only way to entice his presence is to offer sexual activity. If he does not expect an immediate sexual favor, the player will not seek to spend time with his marks. He saves his time for the people in his life that mean more to him.

CHAPTER 6 | EVERYONE'S RECOVERY

Pleasure seeking is directly linked to our pain and is therefore one crafty quantum loop.

Change hurts. Changing your clothes is slightly inconvenient and requires very little recuperation. Changing your kidneys hurts and you need a few weeks to recover. Changing your mind about the man you love? Now that's a doozy and there's no straight forward route to recovery because everyone's heart breaks differently. The goal for someone broken hearted is to simply get past the pain and recover a safe emotional state of mind.

Recovery is a subjective word. By definition, it is the return to a normal state of health, mind or strength and could also mean the process of regaining possession or control of something lost or stolen. Healing by definition is the process of becoming sound or healthy again. Recovery and healing are two words that although intertwined, have two different meanings. On a broad level, the recovery I'm advocating is a regaining of an individual's perception of reality in the pursuit of retaking control of one's mind and body. You must clearly assess your reality in order to make any effective planning. Once you figure out just where you are inside your trouble, you can see more clearly the route to exit. Once you exit, your healing begins. This is equivalent to the hiding away of a physical wound; the exit; after which the restructuring of the damaged cells can begin; the healing and is a process. Once you have exited or removed yourself from the source of your pain, you will then need to maintain a trajectory away from it. You'll also have to apply what you learned to avoid similar situations. This will require your energy and this part is the recovery which is a recapturing of a handle that was lost. The idea is that you continue to engage in healing; perpetually in pursuit to better manage your mind and body; aka recovery. You heal by constantly seeking to regain a handle on life. Full recovery never actually takes place. There can never be a full return to *normal*. If your mind has been changed about something, then you will never fully recover the same particular sentiment you started with. An alcoholic never recovers from Alcoholism because you can't make a normal drinker out of an alcoholic. Their mind has been changed permanently about alcohol and they have to avoid it at all costs. Either he continues to move away from alcohol or he stalls and suffers relapse. Recovery is forever. Healing therefore, is the process that encompasses physical and personal growth. Personal recovery is a constant seeking out of a better outcome.

When processing emotional pain, it is vital that we psychologically put in order the origins of our pain. We must understand the extent and relationship between our emotional and physical connectedness and how often one leads to the other. For example, we obsess over our love object until we call or text them. Their reply or lack thereof hurts which makes us obsess more and the sequence continues. There exists a gradual reducing and accelerating of the velocity of these feedback loops. In other words, once the cycle starts and the thing begins spinning, to make it stop requires a slowing down. Emotions have momentum which means you have to step away and allow a "cool down" period.

Don't expect to solve your emotional problems overnight. To recover from a broken heart, you must first keep juxtaposition far enough away from the source of your pain to allow healing. When your flesh wounds are still fresh, you have to rest the area and apply protective bandages so they have a chance to heal. Distance and time are the bandages that process the pain of an emotional wound. We therefore have to first protect the area of the brain that is affected so that over time it can heal and return to healthy functioning.

In the early stages of emotional pain, consciously, we can be aware of external realities and the changes in our emotional disposition but unconsciously, the decision-making process is being infringed upon. When the shit hits the fan, folks can walk around with a big smile telling everyone and themselves that things are grand but inside they are a nervous wreck. Their unconscious mind is resistant to the change their new circumstances suddenly require. If the underlying issue remains unresolved, life's day to day activities eventually become overwhelming. If severe despondency develops, it can negatively affect an individual's quality of life as well as their loved ones'.

Emotional pain is inevitable. It can lead to depression which is necessary and, in many ways, a healthy phenomenon. Depression is simply the process of giving up something that is loved or familiar. When something interferes with this giving-up process, depression can become prolonged and therefore unhealthy. In these scenarios, our unconsciousness is in battle with our consciousness. That is, the brain will fight to hold onto what is familiar or "how things used to be" and is resistant to accept "how things will be." Often, our brain chemicals are working against us and inhibit change because the brain, once it has experienced loss, struggles valiantly to restore the comfortable conditions it was accustomed to. It uses a feedback loop to encourage you to pick at your emotional wounds by calling or texting your player because it wants to put things back to how they used to be. It is the same reason you pick at a scab on your arm. You want your skin smooth again. The brain has a tricky way of "encouraging" us and if we can recognize these sequences, we can better defend ourselves.

It is demanding to put in the work that comes with change. Our brains are not wired for change in fact the slightest change in procedures at a corporate job can send an entire department flailing. Add a step into the workflow to copy a new party on a weekly email and suddenly everyone is pissed. A person feels soreness in their gut when a lover changes for the worse as the brain labors to continue the effects fantasy has established about the relationship. The unconscious triumphs over the conscious and it often requires a big fight with its neurological pathways to retrain the brain back to sanity. Meanwhile, the individual will suffer through this process in a state of depression since the levels of cortisol and dopamine (among others) have been unexpectedly and negatively altered. The result can prolong the normal healthy grieving process into chronic pathological depression. When this happens, psychotherapy is the best recourse.

One of my favorite readings about pain was from a book called "The Road Less Traveled" by Dr. M. Scott Peck, M.D. The first sentence in this book is simply "Life is difficult." He goes on to explain that once you fully accept this reality, the fact that life is difficult no longer matters. By overcoming the anticipation that life should be easier, one therefore transcends its difficulty and removes the pressure of ease. Essentially, if you are aware a task is difficult, you may not frustrate when you realize it is indeed difficult. Pretty sound stuff. If you're in love with someone who doesn't love you back, don't take it personal. Take it as a lesson on boundaries. Accept that healing and recovery may be a long, hard journey and equip yourself as best you can. So goes the way of life. Reach out to friends, family or a counselor if things feel overwhelming. No one should have to suffer alone and ultimately, you'll end up stronger.

Relationships are not easy. Neither is judging a person's character. We should not fully assert failure to a situation wherein we have misjudged another individual. It is a short and easy route to blaming your poor judgment for someone's unacceptable behavior. Judging character is hard and we'll often get it wrong. We will all experience the pain involved in having our trust infringed upon. It hurts. It happens. It is a natural part of life. There is no one to blame other than the masses. Life is hard. People are harder. This is the cold reality. Relationships are just as much of a numbers game as the lotto but with better odds. Life is a series of guesses and sometimes we misstep, slip and fall. What is important to remember about the inevitability of pain is that we can certainly expect it and according to Dr. Peck, we can decrease our portions of pain simply by accepting it as normal. Emotional pain is something we can either internalize, project onto others or process. We cannot avoid pain but if we process it instead of muddling in it, we can eradicate its devastating effects on our quality of life.

THE DELUSION OF EXPECTATIONS

I have been successful at keeping my personal opinions separate from the science but here, I must chime in emotionally. The lowest point in my healing was one late night with tears on my pillow, writhing in pain as if my body was rejecting its own heart and organs. It hurt emotionally and physically. My sternum felt like it was imploding. I was in utter agony. I could not lie down, sit down, sit up, stand up or lean anywhere. Nothing I did soothed the pain. This suffering lasted unrelentingly for about three hours before I finally fell asleep at around 4:00 am. When I woke, I felt a noticeable degree better but I was still lying flat. "I have to cook breakfast," I thought. If I could just sit up in bed and count to ten, then I could get up and feed my daughters. So I sat up but I didn't bother counting. I just got up and dragged myself out of bed. I was going through a stage of grieving called acceptance. I had finally set aside my fantasies; allowing all the pain of my truth to be realized and it was like torture.

For three hours, I had writhed because I was pushing the issue and telling myself repeatedly, "He does not care." I knew what I knew because in a drunken state, my player had told me outright. "I *don't* care!" he said firmly to my face. He meant it no matter how drunk he was. And no matter how hard I tried, it was impossible for me to *unhear* or *unsee* him telling me the truth. It was and is a memory I can't put away. He didn't care about me. I had to keep convincing myself even though I didn't want to. That is the part that hurts. The point when you realize that yet in your boundless suffering it means nothing to the one you want it to affect the most. Frankly, no one can care as much as you about your pain. Pain isn't transferable. It's yours to manage and I felt all alone facing motherhood with a golden steak through my heart. At my core I wanted to show him my sadness and make him care for me. I wanted him to see what had happened. I wanted to explain it all and change his mind about me. I ended up writing a short email simply telling him that I was hurting. He replied with something like, "It was fun while it lasted." I was devastated because I had expected him to love me and he just didn't.

A woman in my position tends to struggle with the realization that she can be in so much pain over a man that simply is not thinking about her. She may plead with herself saying, "He must feel something. How could he not?" This is a dreadful place to be. Her expectations have suffered a great loss.

The truth is mankind inflicts unrealistic expectations onto itself constantly. This thing called "civilization" has certainly complicated things. It has taught us that women are lesser, gays are evil, sexual women are whores, shy men are weak and that everyone around us should stand, talk and act in a certain way. This idea of what is average or normal among people is one that should be just about played out by now. We expect others to be and think like us yet we are all extremely different, equip with all sorts of contrasting environmental influences, opinions, genes, parents, ideologies and everything down to our choice of socks. Why in God's name do we keep trying to find this perfectly relatable human specimen? Beware and remember Hitler.

In our relationships we also tend to project our reactions, feelings and temperaments onto the people we love. If a person looks, reacts, sounds, or is otherwise too different from us, we view it as negative or dangerous. We should make a cognitive decision to understand difference is okay. If it is safe to say that some men are built for marriage, then it should also be true that some are meant to remain single. Women should understand that some men are not at fault because they are not aspiring to love. If he avoids the subject altogether, he is trying to tell you something; specifically, that you may be in too deep. If he's the type of player that uses the phrase "I love you" without restraint, then you have to stop giving him a chance to say it. Either way, if you are recovering from a one-sided love relationship it means that somewhere along the way, you established an unrealistic expectation.

Flirting is a gamble. A woman can become enamored with a man before she figures out he's not right for her. Sex is a more high-stakes gamble and deciding to love someone is an even more risky ensemble of activities and energies. It is healthier to move through the world cautiously managing your expectations of others keeping in mind that everyone will fail us at some point. The choice is ours on who we will allow to stay in our immediate space. Whether they fail you or grow you, you must decide whether loving them is worth it or whether it is better to take up your heart and give it to someone else. This expectation that people are supposed to feel exactly what you feel on the same timeline as you is preposterous. If you can let go of the expectation that your love interest should experience the same emotions as you, then you can begin to let go of the emotional pain attached to them. You cannot make someone love you no matter how bad it hurts. The longer you stay within this expectation, the longer you will forego your healing. Whether you stay or leave the relationship is a secondary decision. The first decision, letting go of the love expectation, is for you, not him.

ERADICATING IRRATIONAL THOUGHT

Painful emotion triggers irrational thoughts that lead to unhealthy temptations of all sorts. Through a progression, irrational thinking is what leads to revenge, suicide, addiction, manipulation and all types of destructive behaviors.

One of many irrational opinions the mark creates is that the player cares about her emotional welfare. As she begins to accept that she has been played, she may hold onto the hope that he in some small way cares about what she is feeling. In her mind, if he cares about what she feels, it makes sense to share with him when her feelings shift. It explains why she cannot stop herself from sending him texts, emails and calling to explain that she's hurting or happy. Ultimately, she wants to generate a certain response from him. She is seeking some kind of reassurance that he cares and is desperately trying to validate her fantasy and prove that she's right. Unfortunately, she never gets the response she wants while her brain keeps telling her, "You have to make sure before you count him out. Don't quit! Never give up!" The psychosis in this *internal* strategy is that if she gets back in touch with her *external* reality, she will find that her player has already proven careless with her. She has already tested this theory but cannot accept her results. The trouble with this cycle is that each time she reaches out to him, her hope increases and she finds herself working backwards, constantly remolding her external reality. She desperately needs to bring unreasonable thinking into reason.

She is not aware that her recovery is based on her own feelings. Instead, she is building her sense of self-acceptance around his potential feelings. Once she sends a text, she waits for a response. This is when she might read and re-read the message, fantasizing about how her player might react to it. If she can pull herself to diminish all contact with him, it will give her brain the time and space it needs to dissociate with the expectation of his emotions and allow her to assess and mold her own sense of emotional value. She must create a new self-image, apart from his opinion of her. This is accomplished by exhibiting courage to step away from familiarity. If she remains stuck on his interpretation of what is happening, it will be impossible for her to regain her sense of external reality. She must come to a place where his view of her does not matter.

I remember counting the days it had been since I had contacted my player and was on the verge of a small celebration for myself as I approached my first milestone. I had gone nearly thirty days without contact and I was proud of myself. I felt stronger; like I was getting somewhere and could feel my brain trying to repair itself. I was becoming less dependent on the fantasy of him. Then, in the morning on a Mother's Day, he sent a simple text that set me back by some immeasurable degree.

"Happy Mother's Day," he wrote. And that was all it took to throw me into an emotional whirlwind. I cried uncontrollably and intermittently throughout that day; hiding my tears from my daughters. It felt weak and foolish but I had no power over it. I was running away from toxic love and yet this small gesture had punctured me right through the core. First thing in the morning, "Happy Mother's Day" and suddenly, after nearly thirty days of sanity, I was confused and hurt as hell. "Why would he do that?" I begged the universe while drudging through my day, barely getting to anything I had planned. I managed to take my nine and six-year-old for a walk around the neighborhood then cooked dinner and that was it. I fed them cookies for lunch. We had intended on getting on the bus and having an all-day adventure. The kids were lucky I left the house at all.

I was convinced his text had ruined my day but in reality, I had made up my own drama. It was a simple and obligatory gesture; one among twenty some-odd other Mother's Day wishes I received that day. None of the others had meant a thing to me but this one hurt. And it was certainly fair game being a holiday, so I couldn't blame him even though he clearly did not think things through. "Again," I thought, "a lack of consideration for my feelings." It was only a little crazy but certainly irrational. After all, what wise Spring pixie fairy would have whispered into his ear that he should be careful going around making holiday greetings to people all willy-nilly? What was he supposed to do, ask for my permission to send me a greeting? Ok. It was a lot crazy. I was the one with the problem. I had fallen in love with someone who didn't love me and his text was a complete thwarting of my plan to stop thinking about him. The bottom line was I needed to get over it. This was my battle ground and surely there would come more skirmishes to withstand. I finally took a shower at 1:27 pm after feeding the kids a plate of Oreos and just dealt with the shit. I did not reply back to him although I obsessed over the decision all the way until 9:00 pm. I felt like I had survived another day-long merciless battle with my brain and I was tired. I remember going to bed unusually early that night; right at about 9:10 pm. If I had stayed up any longer, I might have texted him back.

Continuing to contact your player will cause your depressive illusion to be prolonged. The more you engage, the more opportunity you'll give yourself to formulate made-up, irrational guesses about what he's thinking. Stay out of his head and don't reply to his communications. This type of restraint is the most difficult part of getting over someone because the brain can remain in a state of stress when it breaks from normal patterns. During intervals of stress, cortisol levels prevent us from making good decisions. A healthy brain makes healthy decisions because it can assess the outcome before applying the best course of action; weighing all angles carefully. When the brain is under stress, the prefrontal lobe (which is our center for decisive thinking) remains somewhat deactivated as the mind simmers in a constant state of fight-or-flight. The brain is not at optimal capacity during periods of deep stress and a woman riddled with heartbreak has great difficulty making sound emotional and relationship decisions.

A mark must elect some serious emotional discomfort for a time so she can bring her thought patterns back to rational levels. This is precisely why this phase of the process is the most difficult. It is much easier to choose temporary and familiar fixes over temporary misery and pain. It is vital that a woman in this position bounce feelings off of trusted friends, family or a counselor so she can gain a better perspective and bypass her erratic way of thinking.

HER PAIN

One of the most pivotal points I make in this book and perhaps more controversial is that a mark's pain starts well before she meets her player and the totality of her behavioral history has caused her to become vulnerable to his harm. If she honestly confronts her pain, she must be unbiased in her self-assessment. She must consider her potential culpability and take a clear look at her dating habits and previous love relationships. Although the player's game consists of one contestant; his self, her romantic relationship required her participation. I bear no burden of responsibility of having my love emotion played with; however
, to honestly address my pain, I needed to understand its derivative. And as my pain bore ancillary feelings of anger, sadness, guilt and shame; it was vital that I assessed the emotional core of what I felt. How had I played a part? Who was I angry with and why? Where did I go wrong? How can I avoid this from reoccurring? I needed these answers so that I could get better.

Becoming caught up in a one-sided love affair is not indicative of a woman's naivety, intelligence or willfulness to succeed in life. It does however give a clear indication that she had unresolved issues prior to seeking her player's approval. Even if she is fully secure mentally and financially; she must vehemently try and solve the puzzle of what caused her to drop her guard; whether due to loss, a temporary mental deficit, insecurity, irresponsible choices or general naivety. This does not mean she has botched the situation; it simply means she must learn something from this experience. Therefore, an unbiased, honest and introspective position is essential; as with anything we learn in life. A child must first learn how to fall before he walks. We learn through pain and discomfort. There is in fact no other way. The mark must be open-minded about her role in the whole mix up and be willing to honestly examine her position. She must stay focused on herself and not her offender's intentions. If she cannot, she is leaving herself susceptible to a repeat.

The user-giver relationship is one that comes in all forms but all point to the same dynamic. That is, they manifest degradation in the value of a person's body or mind. Take for example an abusive relationship wherein physical harm is repeatedly inflicted. There exists a clear degradation of the value of another's body. Mental degradation occurs in codependent relationships wherein one or both participants are inflicting emotional harm by directly or indirectly encouraging dysfunctional behaviors. Herein, there is a clear underrating of the value of the others' emotional welfare and safety by promoting drug use, exhibiting controlling behaviors or imposing verbal abuse; to name a few examples. The mark is the giver and her level of discernment is often skewed towards blaming herself rather than her user, the player. She may focus on what she did to fail at winning his love and this line of thinking is largely centered in what he requires; having no scent of what she requires. This is the selfless curse of the giver. This characteristic is one that has often speckled her life with disappointments and insecurity. It is not her fault that she was deceived and fell in love with a player. It is more likely that her introduction to her player was fringed by intervals of severe to moderate stress related to self-doubt.

The framework of the user-giver relationship is a simple one. The user takes what he can from the giver while giving back as little as possible. The psychology is also simple. That is, the user plays down the giver's sense of worth. The dynamic is one that clearly says the user is entitled to the giver and the giver is therefore unworthy to receive back. It is a power play of two broken spirits each wielding his or her own twisted schema. The giver believes that by giving, she will win the user's gifts. The user believes that by not giving, he will continue to receive from the giver. Both are manipulative agendas. As the giver, her motivation rests in the question of whether she can hold his attention by giving sex, gifts and love. As her player decreases time and energy spent on her, she continues to tolerate him because she has already associated pleasure and reward centers with his approval. This concept plays out fabulously for the player because his approval remains fleeting and inconsistent so psychologically, the mark feels like she's playing the slots in Vegas. Each time she pulls the lever, she waits to see if she wins his acceptance. She is resting her self-value on his opinion of her and this is highly addictive.

After dealing with my player, my pride was the first of my obstacles. Until I realized he had used me, I thought I had been immune to this type of naivety. The concept of the player was like legend to me. After all, I had never been hurt by a player and could not fully relate to this life-long, love-pain that I had heard some women moan about. It was a story I was tired of hearing and it meant nothing. I had figured the women who had been played had somehow played themselves. It was an inconsiderate ignorance to just decide that I was stronger and wiser than the masses.

Apparently, players had no jurisdiction in my life because I could not recall one man who had even come close. I had never been hurt by a man that didn't love me. Most certainly I had encountered a player. Hadn't I? Or it could have been that I didn't care if any of them called me back. I was bold and forthright and still am. If I ended up falling in love, it was with someone who proved they loved me first; never the other way around. I unintentionally played one man into loving me in my bewildered twenties and toyed with others not so severely. At any rate, I had never been scathed by a player. I was cocky in a way and learned a valuable lesson the hard way. After much embarrassment over discovering my vulnerability and suffering deeply over Greggory, my roommate put it to me plainly; "What are you embarrassed for? Not having psychic powers?" She had a point. Putting aside my pride to simply admit that I had no power in the matter helped me get over the "I'm a fool" stage. I wised up when I did which is the best a mark can expect to do.

In weakness, it is important to remind oneself that being deceived does not equal being foolish. No woman or man is immune to being tricked. It may be true that my previous emotional detachment had repelled the games any player may have attempted. When I analyze what had changed, I found there were three distinct variables which lead to my downfall. The first two differences were *timing* and *circumstances*. That is, I met my player at a time when my circumstances had put me in an extremely vulnerable state. Both variables were within my control. The third difference however was mere *providence* which is irrepressible. You cannot control it. It is a kind of fate that only the cosmos allows. When my player encountered me in that state, he decided to make me his mark and I accepted his offer; no matter whether our intentions were fully realized, it happened. I was marked an easy target and he began paying attention to me. This decision was the pivotal providence that I had no control over. This is a revolving rule meaning, if either of the variables had been off kilter, the outcome could have been different. The timing and circumstances would have been irrelevant if the providence of either of our decisions had not been allowed. Perhaps if the cosmos had allowed this providence at a later time and with different circumstance then a different outcome could have been achieved. Albeit theory, my point is, if you have never had your emotions toyed with, count yourself lucky. Hopefully this book will serve you or your loved ones as some protection but also give you a keen awareness that nothing can certify your immunity. Knowing this will help you restore your sense of pride.

Pride aside, the mark is left with a damaged heart and yet her injured feelings are no bother to her player. This is wherein a betrayal feels real to the mark. It may not be that he considered her pain as a foundational step in his plan. He likely didn't give her feelings much consideration at all and took the risk of hurting them so he could experience sexual pleasure. This is an issue of feelings. In the grasp of this kind of hurt, the word "player" is a euphemism. Her heart feels as if the devil himself has conspired to bring her sorrow. It is a deep and compounding pain that is serious. It sometimes leads to health problems, isolation, depression, self-deprivation, addictive relapse or worse suicide. It is a dangerous place to live.

Studies clearly show that when a person experiences the end of a relationship they did not wish to end, the brain exerts the same energy to seek or imagine that other person just as an addict seeks illicit drugs. In fact, one glance at their ex-lover's photograph and men or women in love both experience what mimics drug-craving symptoms; neurologically and physically. These subjects immediately experience increased heart rate, depression, obsession, acute focus, nervous physical behaviors and so on. Just as a drug addict must break the habit, so too must the mark break her addiction to the feelings her player gives her. It is all an illusion. She must train herself to stop masturbating and fantasying about him because each time she does; it opens her emotional wounds deeper and keeps them from healing.

Sensory Confusion

Another very difficult struggle for the mark resides in the complexity of distinguishing between her player's physical presentation and his real self; to reconcile reality and fantasy. She fell in love with the character that he originally presented and the body it was attached to. Now, she opens her eyes and sees the same physical presentation, however the original character has been radically changed. Looking at and listening to him is confusing to both her psychological and neurological selves. In the early stages of her challenges, her psychological self makes the alarming discovery of betrayal and then has the demanding burden of convincing her brain to buy in. The bottleneck is that she desperately wants to convert this new character and the old body back into the condition they were in when she fell in love.

It is amazing how our five basic physical senses influence the brain's perception of reality. At Universal Theme Park in Hollywood, certain attractions are marketed as thrill rides. They are designed to look and feel like roller coasters and through technology trick the brain into thinking they are; even though passengers move mere inches away from their starting point. On one attraction while waiting in line, you walk through a velvet rope down a mechanical corridor. Through a massive steal door, a hissing, steaming rocket ship awaits. You climb into the ship and buckle up surrounded by sights and sounds all counting down to launch. To your front, an enormous screen displays 3D imagery of scenes as they would appear if you were rushing down a flight pad full speed. Plumes of thick smoke rise and with rumbling motors, your vehicle begins to shake. The pavement slowly lowers on the screen and your rocket car accordingly drops; creating that pit in your stomach as if you've just lifted off. Seconds later, you're flying high through a cloud. The visual display, the sounds and feel of roaring wind and engines and the jerks of the coaster car all trick the brain into flooding itself with the same level of adrenaline and cortisol it would release if you were actually flying. That's why we do it. It's thrilling. Synapses work in a network and allow your brain to perceive an external reality when its sensory trigger requirements have all been met; namely sight, sound, smell, taste and touch.

If the mark's player shows up at her door unannounced and plants a hot five-minute kiss on her, she will recall the sensory triggers she felt before she knew he was being dishonest. All her physical senses will be reminded of how her brain reacts to his appearance, sound, smell, feel and taste. Flying at Universal Theme Park, a network of synapses plays again on your senses and activate hormones and muscle groups to prepare you for flight. Your brain cannot tell the difference and when this happens your psychological-self bears the burden of distinguishing between reality and fantasy. Obviously, you're not *really* flying however the mark struggles with the reality that she knows is true, that is, her player is not in love with her. While she may desperately want to believe he is, you are not desperate to believe you are flying in a roller coaster. This type of emotional stress on a theme ride is not present and the experience is therefore processed as positive. The mark, on the other hand, is left with urgency and stress as her brain frantically tries to figure out what is really happening.

The player may not be aware of this scientific phenomenon that pits the brain against the heart but he certainly understands its implications and uses them to his advantage. He is aware that if he can get within earshot, perhaps get close enough to touch her, then he has a better chance at controlling her again; for in his research, this has repeatedly been confirmed. To his credit, when he contacts her in the midst of her deepest pain, within the first few weeks after she has decided to stop seeing him, it does not occur to him that he is in part bringing about or prolonging her psychosis. However, he is exhibiting a certain degree of carelessness as he pursues her without regard for her emotional safety.

Under this type of anxiety, a woman's brain is flooded with cortisol, the primary stress hormone. When this chemical is released, it will temporarily deactivate areas of the brain that promote motivational focuses; sending her into panic mode; a short-term life survival strategy. The brain focuses on how to fix the immediate problem, not solve a long-term situation. It seeks to gratify itself now, not later. Psychologically, she needs levity to make broader decisions about her outcome and wisdom is difficult to come by with cortisol spiking through your veins. The regions she usually commissions to process logic and wise decision making can become clouded and if affected for a prolonged period, she may find herself temporarily incapable of applying rational thought to any of her emotional challenges. We have all felt some form of difficulty thinking when we're afraid or highly stressed. She is in no position to attempt to manage her sensory confusion and if she can muster the strength, she should avoid communicating with him at all costs. This blurring of key sensory centers is truly the root of her grief. If she can overcome this battle with her senses by rejecting direct communication from her player, even if just for a time, she is moving towards emotional recovery.

The rapport between the senses and how the brain interprets them is a stealthy deceiver of the heart. I remember telling myself to take a shower so I could feel better but in reality, I wanted to fix up just in case Greggory came unannounced to my door to finally confess his love for me. It was a fantasy but because I knew that if he showed up and I could see his face, hear his voice, listen to the familiar words then I would believe in him again. I was trying to tie his body back to the character he had first shown me. It would feel normal and therefore better. It was the recognizable brain chemistry that I sought after, not the shower. The brain is a tricky opponent because our senses when mixed with raw emotion, will fight against external reality and bring about a psychosis. Thankfully, knowing what I knew about how the brain works, I was able to catch myself and enjoy my shower with no expectation from him.

SELF-IMAGE

An individual's self-image plays an important role in co-dependent relationships. Once we begin understanding who we are, we create a standard by which we feel others should also live and think. Naturally, humans project what they think about themselves onto other people. It's the reason why a liar always suspects others of lying. Same reason an honest person is always so shocked when they are lied to. They have each expected the world to be like them.

Social psychology is the study of how people are affected by others and just as the brain operates within feedback loop systems, so do social circles. During childhood and as we develop as adults, we learn behavior by observing others. This dictates how we feel people should act, including ourselves. Therefore, personal influences like your family, friends and coworkers as well as social influences like religion, culture and media all play a part in your view of the world and yourself. To think you are not influenced by the world around you is to say a slew of clinical psychologists and pioneering scientists in the field are dead wrong. It is an ambitious and presumptuous endeavor to attempt to walk through life unaffected by the people around you.

If you watched a movie with five friends and all of them loved the movie except you, chances are you may stay quiet as your friends all boast about their excitement in review of the film. Some of us might even change our minds and admit we liked some parts. On the other hand, if you get around a group of people that hated the film like you, suddenly you become passionate about what a shitty job they did filming. This doesn't mean you are a spineless, wishy-washy excuse for a human; it just means you're human. The percentage of people that walk fearlessly through life no holds barred, standing firmly on their every judgment despite popular demand are the slight minority and we consider these exceptional human beings like Geronimo or Harriet Tubman for example. It takes a lot of courage to go against the masses.

By and large, humans form opinions of others based on their self-image and how this image matches up to the rest of the world. Considering your self-worth is an important step in evaluating where you stand in your romantic relationships. If we are not self-aware, we risk dissolving our sense of self. As a result, we may primarily establish our values through others. If the other person does not value us, we must be cautious not to create a thwarted view of ourselves.

In many ways, your sense of self is socially constructed. We find in Asian cultures, an individual's sense of self is surrounded by his community or social affiliations. In these eastern cultures, when asked "Who are you?" people typically referred to their social groups; such as their family or religion to describe who they were. "I am Buddhist," or "I am Japanese," for example. Western cultures, on the other hand, typically refer to their individual emotional values for example, "I am a loner," or "I am an artist." There are stark differences of overall self-awareness between cultures, genders, age groups and race; all of which, according to social psychology, have an enormous effect on how we view ourselves. Whether we primarily identify with our community or through our individuality, it is important to attach positive associations to our self-image, rather than to objects or people. Objects and people change or disappear. Healthy concepts and goals however, have the potential to stay intact no matter the level of loss occurring around us.

Many women across the globe are conditioned to feel secure in their self-awareness when they are connecting to their loved ones and will construct habits of servitude to define who they are as women. "If I keep hot food on the table, take care of the children, keep the house clean and keep my man sexually satisfied, I am a good woman." She may build her sense of self based on her role in her relationship with her lovers and family to the extent that if she loses her family or lover, she finds herself in emotional turmoil, desperately trying to re-identify herself. "If I have no one to take care of, who am I?" This awareness is steeped in her culture.

Typically, the mark has attached her sense of self to a person; her player. If the mark were to take a candid inventory of her love relationships, she may find interesting trends in how she attaches her worth to the people she dates. There is an intrinsic benefit to placing all your life on a timeline. Healing often begins when we put all our good and bad decisions into perspective so we can account for where we went wrong and then reconcile our patterns with the context of our life events. It is as if we scientifically study our own behavior, finding correlations and then attacking our bad habits based on what we come to know. Study your history, understand the direction of your future and keep yourself from making the same mistakes. It is almost impossible to make sense of your challenges until you can get a sense of how they look on a linear scale. Just like scientists who use scatter charts to track data, we must reflect on our behaviors to understand how they started and progressed. Sometimes you can't tell you have a bad habit until you sit down and take the time to think about what you've done and felt along the way. Retrospection is healthy and necessary.

My issues started at age five when some really bad people gave me alcohol before sexually abusing me. "This will make it feel better,' one of them said while handing me my first beer. Sadly, I had no reference of what "better" was supposed to feel like. It all felt horrible. This is where my story of sexual-emotional dysfunction and alcoholism began and from where all my insecurities molded. This is where I decided to place all my self-worth on the interaction my body had with the rest of the world. I had a problem that I had not come to understand until I was almost thirty and had all kinds of self-image issues relating back always to my sexuality. I solved my social rejection issues by drinking and having sex. It was all I knew about acceptance. Sparing the gritty details, when we moved away from that neighborhood and away from those bad people, my problems unfortunately followed me. The first morning in our new apartment I woke up and thought, "Where am I going to get beer now?" I was seven. I went to the refrigerator and poured a few swallows of mom's Reunite right into my mouth then filled the bottle with a little water so she wouldn't notice. My mother was not an alcoholic but kept alcohol in the house so I had a solution. I knew that alcohol made things feel better. The damage was done. I was ripe on my way to becoming an alcoholic whore. Thanks, cruel world!

Going through my heartbreak made me revisit some of my previous emotional victories and reassess my level of maturity; alas at age forty. I had to remember everything. I had to think about all the foolish sexual decisions, abortions, compromising positions and disgusting shit I endured all because I wanted to feel desired. Why? How even? I thought and thought and ultimately, I concluded that I didn't need to blame anyone or change anything other than me and my own perspective. I had to figure out how to stop seeing myself as lesser than others. To do this, I learned that I needed to take time to consider myself. I would spend hours considering everyone else but me. Thank God I feel comfortable enough in my own skin today to actually take care of myself. When I quit drinking alcohol, I stopped seeing myself as I thought other people saw me and began to see me as the person I wanted to become. Self-awareness is an essential key to unlocking your own personal universe, free of everyone else's impartial expectations and limitations.

My self-image was a sticking point that I had trouble accepting. Looking back on my relationship with my player, I felt like I had made a complete spectacle of myself. I was worried that people around me thought I was some kind of desperate whore. Although I found him irresistible, he was not the contemporary portrait of a hot guy. He was an overweight, pigeon-toed, black man with an afro so I assumed the people around us thought I was into him for his money. I felt not only judged by the people he introduced me to but also by him. It was a self-loathing type of insecurity. At one point it occurred to me that maybe he knew of my having been the drunken whore. Perhaps he couldn't allow himself to feel anything for me but failed to have the courage to outright say it. After all, falling in love with a whore is the worst violation of "man code" right? Several times I considered that he thought I was faking my interest in him and was therefore playing me to beat me to the punch. This is psychosis. His actions had nothing to do with me. I was simply his sex toy; nothing more, nothing less. If it had not been me, it would have been someone else. I will never know his reasons for not caring and in the end, it did not matter. The guessing of what others think is the keystone to some types of insanity. This incidentally becomes the predicament of the abused and neglected children of the world. As adults, we sometimes can't effectively process rejection. We are too busy being distracted by our own insecurities because our self-image is in constant strife with the world.

HIS PAIN

While it's important to understand that his mark's pain is an indirect result of his actions, his actions are a direct result of his pain which have nothing to do with her. His pain revolves around his damaged ego and his compelling need to fulfill masculinity through sexual attachments. If he has an inability to care or be cared for, it is a symptom of some other deep hurt or insecurity he has previously suffered. People that serial hurt other people are projecting their pain and insecurities onto the rest of the world. The player therefore projects his thick skin and lack of care onto others. This helps him justify and falsely believe that he is not making a negative impact on people's lives. If the world is as careless as he is, he keeps from being the bad guy.

Ultimately a player's disregard of his mark's body and feelings requires him to answer the question, "How can I justify treating her this way?" His assessments may include, "She's a whore anyway," or, "She wasn't really in love," or finally, "She knew what she was getting into and should not have fallen in love with a guy like me." Incidentally, he's seen this story play out over and over with the same outcome and each time, he has likely suspected his mark would become hurt. He likely knew the moment she arrived at love and that he would string her along unless the relationship came to cause him discomfort. He knows this is how it always goes. At the end of the day, he can easily rest on, "She's putting up with it isn't she? She must like it." The truth is; we should all be careful here. Just because people don't complain doesn't mean they like our behavior. It just means they didn't complain.

His pain therefore, involves a toggling between social expectations, his space of moral action and loneliness; the latter, usually increasing with age. The challenges of proving his masculinity to the world can leave him posturing, projecting, alone and in some cases engaging in all sorts of pathological behaviors. His pain resolves around understanding his space of moral action and how he fits in to the hierarchy of sexual attraction. His masculinity is tied tightly to sexual encounters and considering psychologists report men typically suffer the deepest kind of pain around their associations with sex, this is also the area that is most troubling for the player. He needs to constantly prove that he is sexually desirable and pretending is his only strategy.

Unlike his mark's psychosis which steeps in a false perspective of how connected she is with an individual, the player's psychosis rests firmly in his false perspective of how disconnected he is with individuals. Through repetition, his brain has convinced him biochemically that his combination of social interaction and deceit is at an acceptable level to his moral threshold. In other words, he keeps lying to himself that he is functioning within moral boundaries. He believes there is no emotional, chemical or public consequence to his social interactions and considers himself emotionally indestructible. Therefore, the player's psychosis has very different implications. It causes him to believe he is invincible and free of consequence and pain. His limited perspective may not include his own accountability or the vantage of his partner's. This defines his type of neurosis; that is, even while he is among loved ones, he may feel isolated and out of touch with his emotional reality.

THE SCIENCE OF MORAL ACTION

Scientists are very clever and produce a multitude of tests that can show us what our brain does when we do things; good or bad. We cannot, however, define immorality scientifically. It is not measurable but the results of which are observable. Scientists can observe common behaviors, then make note of their biological and psychological framework. That is, they can test the results of feelings instead of the feelings themselves. For example, I cannot measure how much happiness you have but I can certainly measure how many times you smile per hour. Further, because there is a proven and positive correlation between smiling and happiness, science can confidently assess that if you are smiling a lot, you are more than likely feeling happy with a 20% chance of faking. It is based on a series of averages from a myriad of extremely creative lines of questioning and experimentation. The end result is if you can get the scientific gist of morality, you may be able to more quickly forgive your offender and move on in peace.

By studying schizophrenics and patients with moral impairments after focal brain damage and with the help of fMRI, scientists can detect activities that have identified which systems coerce the space of moral action in the brain. This area resides in a very emotionally driven network inside the ventromedial prefrontal cortex, particularly in the right hemisphere. Often it is a specific dysfunction that shows scientists contrasts which help them determine where to look. When we study the brains of people who perform continual immoral behaviors like killing without remorse, we can see the difference of brain activity to a person who experiences empathy and is naturally appalled by such behaviors. Scientists can therefore identify the brain regions or networks that play some part in the deduction process involved in making moral decisions.

A sociopath develops disconnects with himself and the world during infancy due to maternal neglect and as an adult, seems to make decisions that do not involve the feelings of others or their own. Sociopaths show anomalies in development to particularly the right ventromedial prefrontal cortex and as a result, are unable to choose morality or have great difficulty making moral decisions. This particular area of the brain then becomes examinable to the probability that a person might be either moral or immoral. The trouble with this type of science is that one must define what is moral and what is immoral; a slippery slope when it comes to humans. In fact, it is a careful threading that science must pull off to distinguish "moral" from "better". A careful, creative and smart line of questioning must be applied so as to avoid a way of scientific testing which throughout history, has spawned mass murder of people who were thought to be, by some indefinable degree, *not better*. A morbid shout out to 17th and 18th century scientists because what's done is done and yet some of their evil ideologies and morbid experiments were the frame of reference that helps us decide on smarter questions today. Again, life mimics this constant pull and tug between pain and pleasure as we build strength in our weakness, all to further prove that without failure, one cannot figure out where success starts or ends. Today we know better what questions to ask and define morality around a universal code of moral actions based on "no-harm" and "fairness" rules that motivate a human to actively help and/or refrain from harming other humans.

My point is this, if there be some scientific reason sociopaths, schizophrenics or perhaps 18th century German scientists all behave similarly then consider the person who hurt you emotionally also has some developmental component of his brain that allows him to move about the world with little regard for the things that are common to the rest of humanity. There is a niche for every type of humanoid. There is a reason for everything and no effect can occur without some cause. People are the way they are for a reason and chances are, they were like that before you met them. This is all to help you remove from your emotional framework any hints of guilt, shame, insecurity or otherwise responsibility for someone else's inability to care. Certainly, there are a number of reasons at play; drugs, diet, genetics, environment; take your pick. Nothing you could have done would have likely altered this person's feeling or lack of feeling for you. It could be he couldn't have cared even if he wanted to. We really should not expect people to behave any different than they have behaved in the past. In the end, you'll wind up back where you started. People change behaviors after going through a range of life experiences, not because someone really, really wanted them to. Some people never change. Don't take it personal.

The player, like all of mankind, lives life by certain rules and engages in his own form of justification for whatever he does, right or wrong. We all do it. Birds do it. Bees do it. Even educated fleas do it. No they don't, and apologies to the late Cole Porter. Seriously, the point is, just as a poor person that steals food believes wholeheartedly that he isn't really stealing or perhaps the people he is stealing from must have enough to cover the loss; people justify. The player may stand by the simple rule to never tell a woman he loves her. He may never admit that he has any feelings for his mark at all. In this fashion, he is careful to not initiate the first sexual contact, not lie unless cornered and of course the killer rule of thumb, never, ever, ever actually fall in love. These are his methods of justifying.

Internally he is conflicted and must create rules around his game. He might say, "She fell for me. I never told her I loved her." The truth is the only way he can gain the type of cooperation he is seeking is to appeal to her love emotion. There is no other effective emotion in his pursuit. Whether he is aware, his fundamental scheme is to control her emotionally.

SUBSTANCE ABUSE

Addiction has a direct correlation with the development of social pathologies which is also true of codependent relationships. It was certainly a part of the shaping of the codependency I experienced with my player, the extent of which I will never fully divulge. I will however, pick apart the nature of addiction, how the brain fuels specific addictions and the implications this has on social behavior. This section is meant to contribute to deeper, more meaningful context clues about how drugs and alcohol might be affecting your social interactions. That is to say, if drugs and alcohol are involved, they are affecting your relationship no matter which participant is consuming them.

If generated during an altered state of mind, dynamics in human emotional processing, communication and sexual interpretation create memories of such experiences as figments of our perception; careful not to be confused with figments of our imagination. We have not imagined our experiences while under the influence of mind-altering substances, we have simply perceived them from an imaginary viewpoint; a forced perceptive that is not natural and is often damaging to the brain. If individuals experience life altered, their memories are therefore soiled with a warped perspective of how the world viewed them and how they viewed the world during the mind altered state. In simpler terms, when your mind is altered, everything your brain makes is also altered, including memories and opinions. Therefore, your perception of what you experienced is also permanently altered. The shaping and developing of your brain does not discriminate between a perceived memory and an unaltered memory. It learns by the same process so if drugs are always or often present, the brain will learn to experience life in a specific way. When we then become sober, suddenly the world looks like a strange, twisted and unfamiliar place. Finally, an acute uneasiness sets in and there is no game plan to deal with discomfort without your drug of choice. Panic strikes and our brain reminds us of what it knows can bring about relief; usually some kind of bad habit. Your cravings then become obsession. We obsess over a temporary solution until we become desperate and surrender; giving the brain anything it wants, no matter how dangerous it may be to get it. Drugs, sex, chocolate; anything qualifies. You can become addicted to just about anything. Addictions are a behavioral tactic and treatment isn't so much about the repeated behaviors and substances more than is it about learning to cope without them.

Within a machine, if there is an electrical surge causing mechanical gauges to go haywire, the mechanism cannot effectively collect data. Information is therefore construed or lost in translation. Unlike any invented processing center, our brain has a way of filling in the blanks and putting a solid story together whether it really happened or not. We create a perception of what happened based on how our sensory receptors effectively or ineffectively gather the details of our experiences. Drugs therefore create memory as a figment of our perception. You will only perceive what your drug of choice allows you to perceive. If drugs are a factor in any sexual or romantic relationship, one or both of the parties is bound to become confused. Removing the substance or obstacle that is blurring your experiences will give you a clearer understanding of yourself and the space around you. Then you'll have the resources, strength and clarity to figure out how to cope with your situation.

An individual decides to take drugs to change their state of mind because they don't enjoy the one they currently have. Some argue this new perception is an elevated view. Let me give a word of warning. That is precisely what Sigmund Freud said about how a new strange chemical initially affected him before he went all junky on everybody with his cocaine addiction and spiraled out of control; ruining his career. (By the way, Freud was a mad man and essentially screwed up the science of psychology with his savvy for writing popular and anecdotal nonsense. Do your own research.) The underlying issue is that addiction is the seeking of pleasure to cover emotional pain. All addicts engage in addictive behaviors to cover up existing pain. Life becomes about feeding familiar pleasures, not solving challenges. The universal trick is to train your brain to deal with life, feel all of its emotional values and then step into it anyway without altering your mind through substances. Once one teaches their brain how to cope with stresses and seek pleasure from things that are not dangerous, life becomes much more enjoyable and less complicated.

Addiction is a disease that lies in wait and thrives in secrecy. Hiding behaviors is the fuel to an addict's pain and equally his pleasure and many participants in love relationships with addicts were none-the-wiser. Most of us know nothing about medical or street drugs. We trust our doctors and lovers to tell us the truth. We live in an age where information is so readily available that the responsibility lies today on the individual to understand the difference between what is popular and what is dangerous, what is hearsay, fact, philosophy, or evil. We must fact check everything we learn. For this reason, I will introduce and pick apart two of the most prominent, influential and pervasive offenders. Introducing; two deadly substances that directly or indirectly affected my journey through player hell. Ladies and gentlemen; please, put your hands together for alcohol and crystal meth.

ALCOHOL ADDICTION

What happens inside the alcoholic brain is essentially a very effective and constant taming of the amygdala. The amygdala is a tiny almond shaped area deep inside the limbic system which, if you'll remember, is that strange part in the center of the brain that helps us feel and form emotions. The amygdala is primarily responsible for the dishing out of emotional reactions. Its closest accomplice is the hippocampus (also inside the limbic region) whose job is to store and utilize long-term memory. Together with the amygdala, the hippocampus facilitates complex learning through recollection. These two work as our internal *caution sign*. Alcohol increases a certain hormone responsible for inhibiting the amygdala. This hormone is called GABA or gamma aminobutyric acid.

Now imagine this, Amy (or amygdala) is a total spazoid. She naturally freaks out about everything and sends red alert signals about anything that might potentially be an emotional event. The other regions in the brain cross send signals as it recalls memory from previous sights, sounds, tastes, smells and sensations from the skin to weigh out, in a sort of mathematical equation, whether they should ignore Amy or sound the alarm to the rest of the body. If an individual should spill a glass of milk, it is as if the system asks, "Do we have enough stress signals to start crying over this spilled milk?"

Hippocampus: "Temporal, please respond."

Temporal Lobes: "Roger that Hippo. I need eyeballs on the fridge."

Occipital lobes: "We detect more milk and paper towel rolls."

Temporal Lobes: "Copy that."

Parietal Lobes: "I'm cold and hungry"

Hippocampus: "Pari standby... Negative on cry tactics. Cingulate you copy?"

Cingulate Gyrus: "No PMS to combat or otherwise emotional competitor at this time. Subject is cleaning the milk with concrete plans for action. Mission is accomplished. Blue Falcon. We're gonna dispatch Gaba so Amy can take a ride home."

If the subject should stay calm, neurons send out GABA to keep everyone at normal levels. This chemical keeps people from freaking out when the top of their umbrella gets wet for example or if a bunny happens to hop past them. It inhibits the amygdala and keeps a person calm under normal circumstances. Amy is basically GABA's bitch.

When you drink alcohol, you significantly increase the amount and effects of GABA and so the amygdala takes a back seat until the alcohol is gone no matter what is sad, upsetting or unsettling around us. If Amy is off the clock due to alcohol, our "Spidey" sense is being tamed while GABA is putting in tons of overtime. When Amy reappears, GABA is too exhausted to keep her in check and she turns back into a worrisome fool with nothing to hold her back; aka the depressive hangover.

The continual use of alcohol can therefore create a chemical imbalance that alters the state of an individual's perception of joy, happiness, pleasure, pain and creates an emotional numbness; an atrophy of emotional triggers. Most insidious to this process is the individual's absolute neural instinct and overwhelming need to correct the chemical imbalance. That is, unnatural spikes of GABA become the only way the alcoholic can keep from feeling horrible so they obsess over drinking to feel better. This is called craving and if fed, produces instant relief from suffering. GABA remains on a constant surge-deficit workflow which damages its receptors and exhausts the ancillary systems that have to work hard to fight the effects of this chemical rollercoaster. It is also a most important brain chemical because it is responsible for the production of certain brain cells, the formation and positioning of the brain's neurons and synapse as well as keeping other regions from over or under reacting. GABA is also involved in motor function and is therefore one of the "bad asses" of neurotransmitters because it is extremely important for cohesive neural performance. Damaging this guy's receptors is like pulling your brain apart from the inside out, one cell at a time. Eventually, if you get to drink long enough, "wet brain" will occur. This is the AA nickname for alcoholics whose brains have stopped deducing. These individuals become like walking zombies, unable to react to anything. It's the saddest thing I've ever seen.

Alcohol addiction therefore often plays a huge part in codependency due to the fact that the alcoholic is not skillful at dealing with emotional pain. Alcohol provides temporary relief from pain. When one relies on the concept of covering pain instead of processing it, he robs himself of necessary coping mechanisms and finds himself in a cycle of covering affliction with affliction. When he is drunk, he is okay. When he is sober, he is in pain. He drinks to cover the pain but later finds that his drinking causes more suffering. Nowhere in this cycle is he processing feelings or solving emotional problems. Therefore, the alcoholic player and the alcoholic mark are a magnetic mix because neither of them is thinking straight.

Alcoholism, like all addictions, is a disease of the mind. The word disease, however, is controversial because in this case, diagnosis is not physiological. There is no organism or virus to detect, no means to measure its degree of progression and no form of metabolic testing to pin point its recovery or reoccurrence. In the rooms of Alcoholics Anonymous, members commonly refer to their symptoms of alcoholism similarly; all reporting being physically and mentally ill; complete with headaches, vomiting, sleep deprivation, memory loss, aching muscles, depression, fever, spontaneous urination and unintentional promiscuity among a barrage of other unfavorable and widespread byproducts of alcoholism, not to mention; worried loved ones. According to merriam-webster.com, disease is defined as "a condition of the living animal or plant body or of one of its parts that impairs normal functioning and is typically manifested by distinguishing signs and symptoms." Alcoholism, is clearly linked to malfunction of the brain and body and although its symptoms are spawned by choice, they are symptoms nonetheless, indicating an underlying commonality plaguing millions since the human race discovered alcohol; therefore, a disease.

Why then, are some offended by and therefore actively positioned to thwart the term "disease" from describing the very common and consistent medical phenomenon of alcoholism? After all cirrhosis, the liver damage caused by excessive alcohol abuse, constitutes disease. Schizophrenia is also a disease that cannot be measured medically. Its diagnosis revolves around the detection of symptoms. Perhaps the public's issue is with human choice. Cancer patients do not choose cancer nor do schizophrenics choose their suffering. Emphysema, on the other hand, is a disease caused by smoking cigarettes and is socially accepted as "disease" even though the patient clearly made the choice to smoke. All debates aside, the most important perspective of alcoholism lies in the minds of those afflicted and in the rooms of AA. Its strong fellowship ethics, their concept that the alcoholic is plagued by a malfunctioning and its dedication to the notion that only an alcoholic can help another alcoholic are, to date, the only effective methods of recovery for the suffering alcoholic. I am a sober alcoholic and fully subscribe to the true, tried and trusted methods of Alcoholics Anonymous. AA is what got me sober and I am grateful.

Codependency is a trademark of giver, user relationships even if void of alcohol. This relationship in short, is wherein one person places an unhealthy value on the opinion of another, in order to gain self-worth rather than working through emotional issues to gain self-esteem. When the player is an alcoholic, his innate need to gain worth through the controlling of his sexual relationships becomes a more intent purpose because it is his only form of coping. Since males are biologically designed to secure their masculinity through sex, being an alcoholic, his inexperience at processing negative feelings and applying coping mechanisms leaves him to rely on his primal, unabridged and often brazen character as sexual hunter. With tamed emotions and accountability, it boosts the alcoholic player ego to exercise power over women. He may delight to see them compromised, beg or cry. A codependent player in the throes of alcohol addiction can become emotionally dependent on securing his mark by any means necessary. She is who he calls to make him feel better about himself so interacting with her at his lowest points; while drunk, hung-over or emotionally compromised; is common and causes all kinds of anguish and confusion for the mark. Typically, a woman in love will feel responsible for his well-being and becomes deeply and emotionally involved in his pain. She will do all the tending to the relationship. The alcoholic that is still sick does not make an effort to foster personal relationships. The synergy of drug and alcohol addiction and the game between player and mark is relentless as each dynamic feeds itself into a volatile cycle of pain upon pain; his onto hers.

In some cases, drugs, alcohol and sex are all the player has to look forward to. In his relative perspectives, this is a good life until the drugs and alcohol stop working for him. Eventually, in every alcoholic's life, his options boil down to four; death, mental illness, imprisonment or sobriety. There are no other options as history, statistics and the countless global testimonies of alcoholics have soulfully cried out. The empty chairs in the rooms of AA give its members a somber reminder of why they decided to stop drinking and seeing them; having known the sober alcoholic who used to fill these empty chairs (now either dead, imprisoned or tucked away in a mental institute with wet brain) provides a constant encouragement to stay sober.

METHAMPHETAMINE ADDICTION

It is positively cliché to mention that I used to think I was too smart to get played. Of course, I learned that if the game pieces fell into the right position, anyone could get their feelings hurt. The menacing part was these "pieces" were far more reaching than I could have imagined.

I remember standing outside a bar in Hollywood tongue kissing my player and experiencing a sudden, out of this world rush of feeling, emotion, pleasure, love; everything good it seemed. I actually lost seconds it was so good. The sensation made me feel like the cosmos had brought this man's mouth to me. It was fantastic and yet deep inside I could hear that still yet small voice almost whisper-screaming to my soul, "Run bitch!" This is a true story and I indeed ran. I ran about four feet to my car door and opened it before I realized I wasn't kissing him anymore. My estimation was that I had exhausted at least 2.3 seconds and some involuntary amount of motor exertion to push myself off of his face then walk away to finally reach out and open my car door before I came to. I had no memory of taking one step towards my car. Only through deduction was I able to consider how I maneuvered four feet away. Suddenly, I was exhausted and it felt amazing. Either I was on drugs or God himself had sent this tall black man to visit my mouth. For months, I had pleaded with my maker to explain why kissing him had felt so good. It had felt for a fleeting moment like honest to goodness fate. Turns out, it was an unnatural and unbeknownst dopamine reaction when I absorbed some of the crystal meth that was still in his mouth. What a rip.

Before I knew about his meth addiction, I needed to understand how I was going to walk away from the feelings I enjoyed with him and by the way, how in God's name I had fallen so deeply in love with someone who treated me like a basic hooker? Had I not evolved since my twenties? How had this machine hit me so hard, fast and aggressively? I was smart, somewhat accomplished and mature; yet head over heels in love with what at times felt like a total asshole. Some time passed and as my heartbreak progressed, I researched the brain further, asking different questions yet curiously a hopeful distraction lingered. Amidst it all, I wanted to find out if there was any possibility he had loved me and if he hadn't, what had kept him from loving. In my searching for an answer that ultimately did not matter nor even exist; I discovered my lover's addiction to methamphetamine and the intrinsic wickedness this drug inflicts onto the human brain. Instantly, I was reminded of that night kissing outside the Hollywood bar. Almost two years after the fact, I put it together that the reason he felt so amazing was because I had been getting high nearly every time I touched him. It changed my perspective of him and veritably twisted things up for me.

If your lover is using crystal meth, there are several issues you need to be aware of; namely when you ingest any substance from their body, you are getting high; even if you lick their skin for just a few minutes. Their sweat, saliva and semen will carry methamphetamine several days after consumption. It is also present on their clothing because it crystallizes on everything the smoke touches and can absorb into your body very quickly. Kissing a meth user just after he uses can transfer high enough levels of the drug into your body for you to experience the same effects of stimulation and withdrawal the user feels but to a different degree. To someone who does not use, the effect is enough to tip you over into what feels like pure, boundless love; especially in the female brain. By the way, meth hooks women emotionally and therefore deeper than men because of the way it metabolizes in the brain in relation to other highly emotional components of behavior. In basic terms, because she is more emotional, she is affected more by this very psychological drug.

Some rap artists have referred to this phenomenon as "dope dick" and although the term may seem comical to some and crude to others, it has very serious implications. It should also be considered dope mouth, skin, sweat, hair and clothing. Not only do us parents have the responsibility to assert an anti-drug philosophy onto our offspring, we now must also grant our kids a type of magical defense against this stealthy community of men and woman secretly wielding around their drug infested genitals. These days, unprotected sex not only puts you at risk for unwanted pregnancy and disease; when you have sex of any kind with a person who uses meth, you also risk wreaking havoc on your mental health.

Crystal meth (or Ice) is a new class of drug that is growing in popularity at the speed of light. Cocaine is going away because ice is cheaper and keeps you high longer. I believe initially, I had become addicted to the meth my player exposed me to, mistaking the addictive pleasure feelings for love. It helped me further understand how and why I had fallen so deep and fast for a man who didn't seem to have much respect for me. It was a painful and terrifying discovery. All I could think about were my elementary school aged daughters and what defense they would have against this kind of evil — the horror.

Methamphetamine was originally designed for the soldier with the sole intent to control his mind by removing his sense of accountability, self-survival and to keep him focused on whatever his task. Most notably, Japanese Kamikaze fighters were administered methamphetamine to give them the courage to carry out suicide missions; this after the drug was synthesized in the early 1900s and made more potent; just in time for World War II. Since its creation and migration into recreational use, more than twice the number of meth addicts attempt suicide than die from meth-related illnesses. If the devil himself conspired to create the ultimate weapon against the human race, methamphetamine will have been his greatest tool.

So many neural systems are affected by methamphetamine use that this thing should not be considered a "drug" by conventional standards. This one is something worse and, in my opinion, it should be flagged and labeled into a new class of its own. Crystal methamphetamine is a *super-drug*. Unlike most illicit drugs, the severe and direct complications from methamphetamine use are burdened in the mind, not the physical body. It attacks the central nervous system in a way that causes the brain to neglect its body and moral compass. The typical photos of deranged meth addicts with loosening skin, missing teeth and reports of physical symptoms like death from stroke and severe dehydration – are all ancillary results of a human just not caring for themselves. The real demon behind what meth is lies in its fierce attack on an individual's personal and mental identity by changing *who they are*. It robs an individual of the basic senses of self and survival and replaces these with a thwarted, wicked perception of themselves and the world.

In a nut shell, methamphetamine manages to pretend to be serotonin which fakes the generation of a completely natural sensation; albeit an unrealistic awareness of pleasure. So, the brain is doing what it naturally does, it is just doing it at an incredibly accelerated and unnatural rate. It creates the best feeling you ever had or will have and your brain will never forget it. While you're high, you lose a sense of danger and accountability and gain a sense of kingly confidence and a new, highly curious sex drive. At first, everything feels as natural as the breeze but ten-fold times better. Eventually, a sudden and frightening turn happens and the user finds himself somewhat saddened by everything about himself.

Receptors in the brain are like the traffic lights at the intersections in the brain map we described in the third chapter. In these intersections, cars pull up and the traffic lights tell them when and where to go next. Receptors give the directional cues you use to process routes to your destination, therefore if you hit a road block, alternative measures must occur; namely making a U-turn and finding a different route or foregoing the trip altogether. It may even be decided to give up, abandon your vehicle and walk away. Using meth is like setting the vehicle on fire and walking to your destination wearing a blindfold. Remember, the cars represent our neurohormones. With methamphetamine use, many of the brain's receptors are turned down or off sometimes making it impossible to process a wide range of neurochemical actions like regulating water through the kidneys, physical development and cell formation, the retention of short-term and long-term memories and bonding with other humans; just to name a few. There are many.

While the meth is in his system, it is damaging to dopamine receptors and extended use can cause an inability to feel pleasure. But that's not the worst of it. Crystal has a sneaky way of stimulating and ultimately damaging the HPA (hypothalamic-pituitary-adrenal axis; also see Glossary: *Hypothalamus*). This vital area of the brain does **tons** of important stuff; namely it works within a core network in the brain that regulates how sad, happy, mad or depressed you should become, based on a number of factors involving emotion, observation, memory and cognition just name just a few important ones. These regions all work together to terminate the HPA, so you don't grow too upset, worried, paranoid, depressed or overjoyed. If you permanently damage your HPA, you can no longer regulate these areas effectively. Emotional instability will then endure for life. We learn by reward; that is, through the processing of pain and pleasure. Once crystal meth has ravaged a system, dopamine receptors are damaged or depleted which means some users cannot be enthused, excited or pleasured. This abyss is a surreptitious decline because the victim also loses his points of reference, unable to even recall pleasurable feelings from memory. He can then no longer be introspective. It is therefore typical for the meth user to blame the world for suddenly failing to excite instead of detecting malfunction from within. Subsequently, he uses more meth to compensate; as goes addiction. Additionally, what he is left with is an insurmountable amount of sadness, anger, guilt and shame; all symptoms of the depression that follows because his HPA can no longer receive proper signals from the regions that control his emotion, observation, memory and cognition. It's like being up shit creek without a boat.

This explains several huge pieces to the pervasiveness and dangers of crystal meth. Firstly, meth brains begin failing to perform autonomic nervous system cues that control water retention, the sensation of sleepiness, hunger and their circadian rhythm is bent out of whack. Secondly, once you are hooked, your brain will reject any idea that anything is wrong with you. Those vital warning centers have been turned off. Users may not detect anything abnormal with gritty teeth or eyes. They won't eat, shower, sleep or perform any self-care until the high and withdrawal are gone and the body can go back to acting human again; naturally offended by dirt, danger and discomfort. Thirdly, if you do manage to realize something is wrong, it usually manifests in the type of depression that can lead to suicidal thoughts because often once you realize you have a problem, it is too late to easily solve. This is why more than twice as many users die from suicide than from medical problems related to use. The drug literally tricks the brain out of its instinct to survive and turns on its own body; encouraging its destruction. Sadly, according to countless meth users, this super drug is "pure evil".

Additionally, meth also targets sexual centers and moves an individual into a neural perception of "anything goes" which explains the extremely risky sexual behaviors reported by crystal users. Nothing is unacceptable or taboo if you're high enough which can change a person's sexual context as their experiences continue to shape their brain. Straight men often report feeling "a little bisexual" on meth yet are disgusted by the thought while sober. Some users reported experiencing more "evil" sex on meth. As strategies escalated to make things more exciting; blood, cutting and humiliation were introduced.

Because methamphetamine affects your hippocampus which manages long-term and some short-term memory functions, it disrupts the normal learning process. A meth addict blames everything and everybody else for his meth-related problems because he can't effectively learn the error of his ways. Meth seems to replace the figurative "neural thrown" and becomes King; his predecessor having been his own survival. If you suspect your lover is using crystal meth, you should stop touching them immediately. The best you can be is a support for them if they chose to recover.

MY RECOVERY

My emotional recovery did not start until I made the very difficult and incessantly conscious decision to stop obsessing. It was and still is an ongoing process. Early on, I poured myself into staying busy and yet in those rare but inevitable moments of stillness, I filled my mind with him. Finally, after finishing the section on *Emotional Attachment and Detachment*, it was clear what I had to do. I had to seek a better outcome. I had to seek recovery. My only tools at the time were things like bouncing away thoughts of him, refusing to check social media for pictures of him; going cold turkey on all the masturbating and discontinuing a slew of other really, *really* counterintuitive behaviors. Ultimately, I had an enormous battle to undertake managing what felt like an overwhelming list of *no-nos.*

On top of it all, I had to do away with all the sick reasoning for engaging in such behaviors. I had wittingly and haughtily come to believe it was important to check for signs of his health or well-being; as if that was my responsibility. It was pure, boundless justification to feed "Greggory-tainted" dopamine into my bloodstream; a sneaky, pleasure seeking hoax. By that point, I was clearly cognizant of how I was affecting my neural profiles every time I glanced at a photo of him and had the enormous challenge of applying what I knew and wholeheartedly committing to a strategy. My brain felt broken, damaged and impeded. Void of all neuroscience, I had a problem that was affecting my day to day responsibilities with my children and the company I owned. Reluctantly, one year in April, I stopped everything. I tearfully ceased all contact with him, stopped intentionally listening to sad love songs, quit hoping he was hurting too or at least cared that I was suffering. Instead, I chose to endure the fullness of my pain. I felt like a drug addict choosing a very raw and isolated withdrawal. Surely, no one could relate to this nonsense. "How embarrassing," I thought.

Although it was not easy, once fully committed, eradicating these *peripheral behaviors* were relatively less difficult. Physical boundaries were easy. No doing this or that. No moving my body in a way that will cause me to see his face. The *psychological behaviors* were my greatest peril. For example, there were moments when I fought hard against an onslaught of fantasy, visualizing his face and genitals, fantasizing about bumping into him and rekindling the flame or friendly exchanges and deep loving conversations. I would catch myself several minutes deep into a fantasy scenario, enjoying those familiar pleasure triggers before seizing reality to literally say aloud to myself, "Stop doing this! Your brain is desperate for the recognizable neurological profile associated with him." For me, this worked. Thank God I'm a nerd?

Before long thoughts of him, although intense, grew fleeting. Each time his face or name presented themselves, the rush of dopamine would be a mere but inevitable reminder; that soft pinch at my heart strings. Like my mother had forever boasted, "Practice makes perfect!" I kept practicing bouncing thoughts of him away. Repetition was the key. I was unrelenting and over some perfectly acceptable season of time, I mastered how to get my dopamine fixes elsewhere. I used healthy objects of fantasy and began visualizing myself as a happy single mother, secure in her career and self-worth and thoughts of him became relatively brief and less frequent. The finest things and feelings in life became my new obsessions. I fantasized about the success of my business and finishing my book. It felt strange, selfish and at times obligatory but eventually it helped reshape my perspectives and I began accepting myself, my past and my future despite what my culture and personal insecurities were telling me. It is unfortunate people have to go through hell to get to peace but the cosmos has a way of putting a fire under your butt to get you out of a mess. We live. Therefore, we learn.

I've heard people say that one, "cannot control their thoughts," but this concept is absurd and immature in my opinion. It doesn't make an ounce of scientific sense. I cannot recall where I first heard the more accurate proverb; "You might let a bird land on your head but you don't have to let him build a nest there." It is true that you cannot keep fleeting thoughts from entering your mind but you can certainly make a cognitive decision to cease entertaining them. It is a learned skill that increases in strength and effectiveness with repetition. Once you begin to eliminate the peripheral behaviors, you will find it easier to manage your psychological thought processes and regain your emotional stability. Luckily for mankind, the brain already starts doing some of the recovery work for us.

I remember when my emotional challenge came into a manageable space. My neurological and psychological selves began to readily merge into sharing one accord. The push and shove between dopamine and cortisol had become less contentious and the air was finally lifting. I found an elusive space in my spirit that allowed me to be okay with loving him. I loved him. There was no undoing that and I needed to be able to smile about the love I felt and leave it free of expectations from him or me. He did not love me back. This was my reality so I entertained being okay with it all.

Instead of holding on to any hope that he would ever love me, I set out to carry on with my life, excluding him; but loving him from afar. Turned out, this required way less energy.

Nonetheless, the pain after I ended my relationship became extremely intense and I dare try and limit its description to a mere paragraph. Considering the uniqueness of the relationship, to thoroughly explain the personal account of this kind of mental and physical anguish would require another complete book dedicated solely to subject. To pick apart all the separate twists and turns, victories and failures, tears, choked back tears, cursing, praising, the grinding of teeth, the holding onto my chest, the remembering to breathe, the forgetting to eat and so on – to describe fully what happened, it would unquestionably oblige a type of energy that I no longer believe I possess. The only purpose in giving this window into the pain I experienced is to highlight for the reader, on some relatable level, the gravity of seeing an end in sight. There is a power beheld when we realize we're standing at the threshold of our greatest battles and in the horizons, we finally sense the scent of relief.

It wasn't easy. There were ups and downs of course. Three days would fare good then two bad; one good, then four horrible days of crying and regretting. There were no patterns and at first, I could not detect any success. I floated aimlessly between incredible despondency and being exuberantly motivated and it was exhausting. (See Glossary: *Cingulate Gyrus*) Finally one afternoon sitting at my desk, I felt the warm sunshine on my right arm anew. It felt warmer and the light shone brighter. I became entranced and focused on the beauty of my light brown arm hair before it dawned on me that it had been longer than I could remember since I had cried about him. I could not recall the last time I had felt sad over him. It had not occurred to me until that moment that I had been getting somewhere and it was marvelous. "I'm getting better," I whispered aloud. I felt a new kind of strength that reminded me of the first time I had to kill a spider after the divorce all by myself. It felt like victory and all it took was a little warm sun and a few arm hairs to remind me of myself. At that realization, I shed three or four tears of joy and celebrated in a quiet moment for my small victory and my big future. Health and freedom were in sight. Each of us will experience our own kind of pain and joys. Truthfully, with my player, I had an awful lot of both.

The other underlying element which required a final analysis was our financial relationship; that is, when I needed help, all I had to do was ask. I asked only as often as I absolutely needed to however, as time progressed, I found myself becoming less responsible with what little money I made from my fledgling business and child support. The safety of knowing his help was a phone call away created an unhealthy indifference in my handling of finances. Subsequently, a strange lethargy lingered over my finances for the time I accepted his help. When I severed contact, my account was almost a thousand dollars overdrawn and I was under incredible stress. Admittedly, prior to making the decision to stop seeing him, I had spent an entire month banking on asking him for $2000 to get me out of trouble. Despite my plans and just before rent was due, I dared to step into the elevation of self-determination and with great trepidation; I ended things by sending him an email. Altogether, I cranked in, fully focused on my business model and made it through May, then June and continued an acceptable quality of life for my family without his help. I sacrificed big time and I found my independence again. Of course I did.

In total and typically in $1000 to $2000 transactions, he had transferred over $20,000 to my bank account and handed me $420 in cash during the four years we were romantically involved. That averages $425 per month towards my meager lifestyle. All told, no matter his intentions, clearly the cosmos had divinely intended that he help me through those early years after my very financially devastating divorce. Strangely, the figures work out over four years to about $212 a blowjob; about the price of a moderately expensive hooker. Why these figures were worth calculating in the first place is left to be interpreted.

At last, within a few weeks of some hard and honest talks with myself and sticking to my plan, I was able to go one step further outside resisting actions related to him. I also began successfully resisting temptations to crave him mentally and it made me feel whole again. Although still very deep in pain, writing this book was an incredibly therapeutic distraction. It felt as if I was writing the mother of all journal entries. Naturally I found it too difficult sometimes and had to break from writing for days or weeks. But as I researched and studied, weaving in and out of strength, I began to paint a picture of just what had happened to me and him. By the time I was ready to publish; I was well on the way to healing and had learned how to stop relying on the acceptance and improvement of others. It became important to lean on the acceptance and improvement of myself. I knew our relationship had been happenstance. I had been in the right place at the right time. We met. We had fun. I got hurt. I learned a lot. I don't know if he learned a thing and I am okay with that.

Gaining the knowledge about my brain was monumental in my own self-discovery. I learned that my bad habits were simply a response to neural impulses and this knowledge made them easier to battle. All told, the reasons I came to learn such extensive details about the brain are insignificant because through it all, I gained an invaluable treasure. Our brains are our masters and we must answer to our masters' will. It is a great freedom from self and sorrow to understand how and why you and the world feel pain. Understanding it gives you a power over pain and lessens its sting. I can still cry for the helplessness I feel about the devastated world around me but the tears are a means to push me into hope and action rather than disparity and stagnation. It allows me to love an evil world and an unscrupulous lover; neither of whom loved me back and yet strangely today, neither can hurt me very deeply. As long as I continue to practice my ideologies, being aware of the science of behavior, the choice between loving and despising individuals becomes an easy one. I choose love. In fact, I can still manage to think of him and smile after all; my brain will be forever tied to him. Today, however, I am careful not to give him anything that he can squander.

GLOSSARY

The sole purpose for this short glossary is to cover parts of the limbic system that were not thoroughly covered in chapter three. The emotional limbic system, located at the base of the brain, is made up of the following six areas:

Amygdala

The *amygdala* is a small, almond shaped formation almost center brain and it evaluates and manages our emotions; sadness, happiness and fear among others and is responsible for "fight or flight" when we are met with danger. It processes learning on the basis of reward and punishment through pleasure and pain and is also involved in the formation of memories, especially those laden with emotional value.

Basal Ginglia

The *basal ginglia* is a group of nuclei located on both sides of the thalamus (See *Thalamus*). These nuclei arrange themselves above the limbic system and all the way through to both the occipital and temporal lobes. Each group, having their respective purposes, manages a wide variety of neural functions ranging from riding a bike to recognizing when something in your life is wrong and needs to change causing us to take a shower when we're dirty or lock our doors before bed, for example. Nuclei in the basal ginglia also send and receive messages to and from the prefrontal cortex which contributes to personality. This area of the brain, when damaged or operating abnormally, can contribute to obsessive compulsive disorder

(OCD), Parkinson's disease, Tourette's syndrome, Attention Deficit disorder (ADD), depression and schizophrenia to name a few.

Cingulate Gyrus

The *cingulate gyrus* covers the corpus callosum (which transfers motor, sensory, and cognitive information between the left and right brain hemispheres) and is highly significant to the connection of the effects of behavior to the motivation necessary for learning. It uses a system of positive and negative emotional responses to encourage cognitive avoidance of future negative emotional pain. This is our motivation center and it manages the associations between memory and emotional pain to encourage fear and the prediction of unpleasant consequences. After personal loss, this area usually kicks in with a force to help us get through the emotional pain. Most people therefore toggle between feeling sad and highly motivated while recovering from loss.

Thalamus

The *thalamus* snuggles comfortably underneath the amygdala and is solely responsible for carrying sensations from body surfaces to the cerebral cortex and relays 98% of sensory impulses required for observation; namely sight, taste, hearing and touch. Smell is the only sensory information that the thalamus does not handle. This sensory path is different and uses olfactory bulbs located in the back of the nose which are also linked to our limbic system. Since the thalamus is in very close proximity to the amygdala; emotion is closely linked to physical sensation.

Hippocampus

The *hippocampus* resembles the shape of a seahorse and is nuzzled between and wraps around the amygdala. It mainly regulates associations with long-term memory. Since scientists know emotional values are closely linked to memory, the hippocampus is thought to be the center of emotion. It also regulates autonomic nervous system functions like breathing, heartbeat and digestion.

Hypothalamus

The *hypothalamus* is located under the thalamus, hence its name, as "hypo" means under and it handles production and maintenance of many neurohormones. This is a pretty important job. This means it essentially generates our reactions or sensory impulses and it also synthesizes these hormones, or "translates" them into messages our body understands. The hypothalamus regulates thirst, hunger, body temperature, fatigue, sleep and some very important aspects of parenting and human bonding behaviors among other functions. This region is very special because it essentially is the referee, pioneer and overseer for all other regions of the brain. Methamphetamine use creates a huge and permanent threat to this area of the brain.

RESOURCES

BOOKS

1. Brizendine, Louann, M.D. "The Female Brain" Broadway Books New York, an imprint of The Doubleday Broadway Publishing Group, a division of Random House Inc., New York, NY, 2006. 14, 21-22, 33, 36, 38-39, 43-44, 46, 49-53, 71, 161-182, 186.

2. Brizendine, Louann, M.D. "The Male Brain"; Broadway Books New York, an imprint of the Crown Publishing Group, a division of Random House Inc., New York, NY, 2010. 9-67, 72-81, 95-102, 143-144.

3. Gurian, Michael, Dr. "What Could He Be Thinking?: How a Man's Mind Really Works." St. Martin's Press, New York, NY, 2003. 9-13, 29-31, 33, 45-48, 50-53, 55-57, 59, 61-62, 64, 179-180, 183.

4. King, Brian, Dr. "The Laughing Cure: Emotional and Physical Healing - A Comedian Reveals Why Laughter Really Is the Best Medicine." Skyhorse Publishing, New York, NY, 2016.

5. Eds. Decety, Jean; Ickes, William J. "The Social Neuroscience of Empathy." A Bradford Book, MIT Press, Cambridge, MA, 2009. 6-9, 74, 115, 119, 128, 133, 188, 191, 200, 206, 216-217.

6. Gray, John. "Men Are from Mars, Women Are from Venus: The Classic Guide to Understanding the Opposite Sex." HarperCollins Publishers Inc., 1992. 143-164.

7. Lambert, Kelly, PhD. "The Lab Rat Chronicles: A Neuroscientist Reveals Life Lessons from the Planet's Most Successful Mammals." Penguin Group (USA) Inc., New York, NY, 2011. 49, 137-138, 143, 161, 195, 228.

8. Pinker, Steven. "How the Mind Works." W. W. Norton & Company, Inc. New York, NY, 1997. 5-10, 15-18,113-114, 131, 183-184, 271, 373-374, 563.

9. Edelman, Gerald M., Dr. "Second Nature: Brain Science and Human Knowledge." Integrated Publishing Solutions, United States of America, 2006. 20-21, 32, 36-38, 42, 92.

10. Keestra, Machiel. "Sculpting the Space of Actions Explaining Human Action by Integrating Intentions and Mechanisms." Institute for Logic, Language and Computation, Universiteit van Amsterdam, 2014. 203-226.

11. Eds. Sternberg, Robert J.; Weis, Karen. "The New Psychology of Love." (Chapter 5) Fisher, Helen. *The Drive to Love: The Neural Mechanism for Mate Selection."* Yale University, New Haven & London; 2006. 87-107. http://www.helenfisher.com/downloads/articles/15npolve.pdf;

12. Knapp, Caroline. "Drinking; A Love Story." The Dial Press, Sold by: Random House LLC, 1999.

13. Ms. T. "The Player Slayer: The Pocket Guide to Jamming the Player's Game." Kindle Edition published by Agate Chicago, 2006.

14. Rinehart, Paula. "What's He Really Thinking?: How to Be a Relational Genius with the Man in Your Life." Thomas Nelson Inc, Nashville, Tennessee, 2009. 34-38, 77-81.

STUDIES

1. Toledano, Rachel PhD; Pfaus, James PhD. "The Second Arousal and Desire Inventory (SADI): A Multidimensional Scale to Assess Subjective Sexual Arousal and Desire." Wiley Online Library, 2006. http://onlinelibrary.wiley.com/doi/10.1111/j.1743-6109.2006.00293.x/abstract

2. Wolf, Oliver T.; Schommer, Nicole C.; Hellhammer, Dirk H.; McEwen Bruce S.; Kirschbaum, C. "Psychoneuroendocrinology" (Volume 26, Issue 7 October 2001), "The relationship between stress induced cortisol levels and memory differs between men and women" FIRST Institute of Experimental Psychology II, University of Duesseldorf, SECOND Germany; Center for Psychobiological and Psychosomatic Research, University of Trier, Trier, Germany; THIRD Laboratory of Neuroendocrinology, Rockefeller University, New York, NY, USA, 2001.   http://www.psyneuen-journal.com/article/S0306-4530(01)00025-7/abstract

3. Vanderbilt University. "Different Parts Of The Brain Handle Fantasy And Reality" by Published by Vanderbilt University; "They look very similar behaviorally, but it turns out they use completely different neural circuits and the brain doesn't know how to put them

together." 2002. *illustrates studies conducted before we knew fantasy and reality are handled in reverse.* https://www.sciencedaily.com/releases/2002/03/020329072629.htm

4. Mendez, Mario F. MD, PhD. "The Neurobiology of Moral Behavior: Review and Neuropsychiatric Implications." Published in final edited form as; 14(11): Author manuscript; available in PMC August 29, 2011, CNS Spectr., November 2009. 608–620. https://www.ncbi.nlm.nih.gov/pmc/articles/PMC3163302/

5. Gallese V., Fadiga L., Fogassi L., Rizzolatti G. "Action recognition in the premotor cortex." Oxford Academic: Brain – A Journal of Neurology, 1996. 119, 593-609. https://academic.oup.com/brain/article/119/2/593/382476

6. Eds. Freund H.J., Jeannerod M., Hallett M. "Higher-order motor disorders: from Neuroanatomy and Neurobiology to Clinical Neurology." Oxford University Press, New York, NY. http://www.liralab.it/projects/mirror/docs/SecondYear/papers/Rizzolatti%20and%20Fadiga%20(in%20press).pdf

7. Van der Meij, Leander; Almela, Mercedes; Buunk, Abraham P.; Fawcett, Tim W.; Salvador, Alicia. "Men with elevated testosterone levels show more affiliative behaviours during interactions with women." The Proceedings of The Royale Society Publishing; Downloaded from rspb.royalsocietypublishing.org; June 1, 2011. https://www.uv.es/labnsc/art%20labnsc/2012/van%20der%20meij%20et%20al.,%202012%20proc%20r%20soc%20b.pdf

8. Helion, C.; Ochsner, K.N. Neuroethics. "The role of emotion regulation in moral judgment." Springer Netherlands and The Department of Psychology, Columbia University, New York, NY, 2016. 5-6, 23-26. https://doi.org/10.1007/s12152-016-9261-z

9. R. Cavalcanti. "The Neuroanatomy of Sex and Love." The Journal of Sexual Medicine, Cesex, Salvador, Brazil, 2011.

10. Walum, Hasse. et al. "Genetic variation in the vasopressin receptor 1a gene (*AVPR1A*) associates with pair-bonding behavior in humans" Proc. Natl Acad. Sci. 105, 14153–14156 (2008). http://www.pnas.org/content/105/37/14153

11. Young LJ, Wang Z "The neurobiology of pair bonding." Nature Neuroscience volume7, 2004. 1048–1054. Download available at https://www.nature.com/articles/nn1327

ARTICLES

1. Website: Sociopath X "Sociopathic Personality Disorder and Types." Depression D (depressiond.org), 2010-2011. http://depressiond.org/sociopath-sociopathic-personality-disorder/

2. Marsh, Jason. "Do Mirror Neurons Give Us Empathy? Neuroscientist V.S. Ramachandran explains what mirror neurons tell us—and what they don't—about empathy and other skills." The Greater Good Science Center at UC Berkeley, March 29, 2012. https://greatergood.berkeley.edu/article/item/do_mirror_neurons_give_empathy

3. G. Zuloaga, Damian; Johnson, Lance A.; Agam, Maayan; Raber, Jacob. Journal of Neurochemistry, "Sex differences in activation of the hypothalamic–pituitary–adrenal axis by methamphetamine." Wiley Online, February 10, 2014. http://onlinelibrary.wiley.com/doi/10.1111/jnc.12651/full

4. Laslocky, Meghan. "This Is Your Brain on Heartbreak: Why does getting dumped hurt physically? Meghan Laslocky explains where that feeling comes from, and what it's good for." The Greater Good Services Science Center at UC Berkely, February 15, 2013. https://greatergood.berkeley.edu/article/item/this_is_your_brain_on_heartbreak

5. Arciniegas, David B., M.D.; Kaufer, Daniel I., M.D. "Core Curriculum for Training in Behavioral Neurology & Neuropsychiatry." American Psychiatric Publishing, Inc., 2006. http://neuro.psychiatryonline.org

6. Greenberg, Melanie, PhD. "This Is Your Brain on a Breakup." Published on Psychology Today website, March 29, 2016. https://www.psychologytoday.com/blog/the-mindful-self-express/201603/is-your-brain-breakup

7. Kessler, Ronald C.; McLeod, Jane D. "Sex Differences in Vulnerability to Undesirable Life Events." Published by American Sociological Association, 194. Vol. 49, No. 5, 620-631. https://www.jstor.org/stable/2095420?seq=1#page_scan_tab_contents

8. Young, Larry J. "Love: Neuroscience reveals all." Nature; London Vol. 457, Iss. 7226, Jan 8, 2009. 148. https://www.nature.com/articles/457148a

9. Firoozi, Mahbobe; Azmoude, Elham; Asgharipoor, Negar. "The relationship between personality traits and sexual self-esteem and its components." The National Center for Biotechnology Information and the Iranian Journal of Nursing and Midwifery Research, Copyright 2016. https://www.ncbi.nlm.nih.gov/pmc/articles/PMC4857655/

10. Makini, Brice. "Sweat, Saliva, and Smells: How Sexual Desire Overpowers Disgust." Science/Tech; Medical Daily, Sep 13, 2012. http://www.medicaldaily.com/sweat-saliva-and-smells-how-sexual-desire-overpowers-disgust-242503

11. Betchen, Stephen J., D.S.W. "The Player: A sometimes unfair label of men in the dating world." Published on Psychology Today website; August 6, 2012. https://www.psychologytoday.com/blog/magnetic-partners/201208/the-player

12. Hebron, Allison. "How Is the Level of Testosterone in the Blood Controlled?" Livestrong.com website, August 14, 2017. https://www.livestrong.com/article/270042-how-is-the-level-of-testosterone-in-the-blood-controlled/

Made in the USA
San Bernardino, CA
24 July 2019